CONTENTS

PREFACE

My work as a psychiatrist has brought me into contact with two of the key behavioural sciences which, under the umbrella of psychology and psychiatry, have contributed a major element to the revolution in man's understanding of himself as an individual, both in one-to-one relationships, as a member of a small group, for example in the family and as a constituent of the bigger group in the local and national community. Psychiatry belongs to the world of medicine in that its chief concern is the restoration of mental health when this is disturbed but it relies on psychology, its handmaid, which is concerned with the science of the mind or, less controversially, the science of behaviour. Psychology covers a number of specialized fields such as normal, abnormal, animal and human. In human psychology it is divided into that of children, adolescents and adults and it can be further subdivided into industrial, educational and clinical. The most familiar aspects of psychology, apart from the concept of measuring intelligence in the form of I.Q., are the famous systems of thought based on the works of Freud, Jung, Adler and the successors of the fathers of what has come to be called − dynamic psychology. Dynamic psychology is concerned primarily with feelings, emotions and instincts and their mechanisms of operation in the human personality. The affinity between this area of psychology and faith is close, linked through the significance of affectivity in initiating and maintaining relationships between man and man, and man and God. This link provides also a clue to my own and other behavioural scientists' continued belief in God, not as an act of despairing defiance but as the expression of the conviction that as man uncovers successive layers of his complex nature, with the help of science, we are privileged to approach a little closer through 'seeing', 'touching', 'feeling' and 'living' it, to the mystery of God, in whose image man has been created. Thus, far from reacting to science as a threat to faith, it is possible − indeed necessary − to welcome its methods as a legitimate means of realising an expanding awareness of the meaning of God's infinite wisdom and love, in the wonder of his creation. All science, but the behavioural sciences in particular, is potentially capable of becoming faith's ally, illuminating the statement in Genesis (1:31) − 'God saw all that he had made, and indeed it was very good.' The danger lies in the possibility that man will not be content to see, comprehend and accept creation but will try to improve it without reference to its

vii

founder. In this lies disaster.

These essays were written over a period of five years. They were not prepared for collective publication and had to be rearranged for this. Some have not been published before. Thus they do not represent a detailed, cohesive organised cycle of human experience. They were written for different occasions, addressed to different audiences, some of whom could follow the talk with a live dialogue, not possible with articles written specifically for journals. Thus there are inevitably a few repetitions.

The religious who meet regularly at Spode House at the beginning of each year have asked repeatedly for a permanent form of presentation, a request which has also been expressed elsewhere. I resisted this for a long time because I did not feel that these contributions amounted to more than an outline, an excursion, a reconnaissance between theology and psychology. I am without any formal training in theology. My theological considerations are personal and subjective. I would welcome the views, be they positive or negative, of trained theologians.

Despite the obvious theological limitations, all the essays were written with certain convictions, some would say bias, clearly held. The first is that all Christianity, in common with the whole of Western society, has paid too much attention to man's intellect and too little attention to the inner world of feelings. That Catholicism in particular has coupled this with an excessive preoccupation with law emphasizing activity outside man and too little experience inside. And that a combination of the abstract and the legal has removed man's religious focus from the immediacy of everyday experience which has been trivialised by obsolete and irrelevant notions, symbols and ritual. I hold in particular that the present decline of Christianity is due to its inability to act as a catalyst of love in everyday social and pyschological experiences in a world that is desperately eager to experience sanctification in the depths of its being.

Psychology, with its varied approaches, is eminently suited to assist in this predicament. Love is considered in terms of the development of the personality and in such concepts as relationship, self acceptance, self esteem, realisation of potential, fullness, affirmation, wholeness and other dynamic elements. Since the essays were not concerned with technicalities, either theological or psychological, definitions were mostly eschewed. This suited my style of approach which is strongly influenced by the view that once definitions enter into a situation, people spend much more time with the intellectual gymnastics over the details rather than with grasping through feeling the essentials of the point of view presented. There is, of course, a place for careful evaluation of the meaning of technical terms but this is best dealt with in other publications, textbooks or technical journals.

Many of the essays concern my special interest in ways of living and experiencing ourselves, i.e., of marriage and the single state, of religious life and the priesthood. I have attempted to link them as part of a continuum in which there are marked similarities of human needs, capacities to relate and possibilities of fulfilment.

Throughout there is an emphasis on the psychological nature of man, particularly its dynamic aspects. But the main concern has been to describe in empirical terms the meaning of love in a whole range of ordinary and common human situations, many of which have been known only through the rules and regulations surrounding them. The penetration of everyday experience with the concept of love as experienced by the participants has been uppermost in all the writing.

There will be, of course, disagreements about the use of the word love to describe particular aspects of experience. This, however, is infinitely preferable to those boring discussions as to whether a definition is acceptable or not. Since love is the nature of God, everything which might help us to identify and experience love in our lives is a step towards realising that fullness of self which is created in the image of God.

J. Dominian
September 1973

ix

This first essay, which was given to a liturgical conference, stands on its own. Here an attempt is made to describe universal characteristics of love, linked to personal integrity found in the life of Christ and expressed in an increasing endeavour of fulfilment in our own. This essay was constructed by transferring some of the discussions in dynamic psychology to the life of Christ and then reflecting them back on our own. The points made here recur throughout the book because the understanding of the nature of love in various human situations is the motive behind all the essays.

HUMAN AND DIVINE LOVE

The subject of love is of universal interest, has engaged the attention of many since time immemorial and will continue to do so. It is of particular interest to Christians who claim that God is love. If this be true, and our faith tells us it is, then no other subject is of comparable significance.

It is for this reason that I am beginning this paper with a brief personal credo which can be stated simply. If Christianity finds itself in a situation in which few are really concerned with its survival and many find it irrelevant to their lives, I believe that, in the final analysis, this is so because Christianity has failed in its fundamental mission which is to be the catalyst of love in the world. After all possible causes for its present decline, such as its internal disunity, its obsolete language and liturgy, its authoritarianism, its pessimism over sexuality, the disarray of its structures, the anachronism of much of its habits and its legalism have each been exhaustively examined, I believe there is left one enduring and irreducible reason which is succinctly stated by St. Paul:

> If I have all the eloquence of men or of angels but speak without love, I am simply a gong booming or a cymbal clashing. If I have the gift of prophecy, understanding all the mysteries there are, and knowing everything, and if I have faith in all its fulness, to move mountains, but without love, then I am nothing at all. If I give away all that I possess, piece by piece, and if I even let them take my body to burn it but am without love, it will do me no good whatever.
>
> Paul 1 Corinthians 13: 1-4.

To paraphrase this notion it can be said that the Church can acquire a most efficient system of collegiality, decentralisation, freedom from obtrusive authority, settle the issue of celibacy of the priesthood and that of birth control, etc., to the satisfaction of everybody and still remain a voice crying in the wilderness because all these issues leave our neighbours bored and disenchanted. And my sympathy is entirely with a great friend of mine who, after listening to this grand tale of reformation, or rather possible reformation, grunted 'So what?' Is Christianity really going to make an impression through exercises in democracy and freedom? The sceptics can point out that the principles of democracy were enunciated in ancient Greece and it is too bad that it has taken two thousand years for the Church to discover it has a problem and to try to do something about it. The cynics will go on to quote, with puckish delight, from the first chapter of Genesis, the passage about God seeing all he had made and finding it very good. They may even throw in Solomon's Song of Songs for good measure. And again it is too bad that Christianity has had to wait two millennia to recognize the intrinsic value of sexuality. Indeed, it is not only pitiable, it borders on the pathetic, given the amount of illumination which the Bible has shed on the subject.

We need to do much better than to have two reformations, one in the sixteenth century and one in the twentieth, to impress a world that has touched down on the moon and is already on its way to the other planets. Ecclesiastical news which produces seismic seizures in Rome is translated into a mere journalistic ripple in a world that is punch drunk with its own technological and industrial achievements. But this world which seems to have everything lacks one thing, namely, the ability to ensure that its anger, hatred and destructiveness do not prove greater than its capacity for peace, love and real creativity. However, the command to love precedes our discussion on democracy no matter how important the latter may be. The words of the 18th verse of the 19th Chapter of Leviticus which state categorically that we have to love our neighbour as ourselves are again magnificently echoed in the 4th Chapter of the First Epistle of St. John where we read:-

No one has ever seen God but as long as we love one another
God will live in us and His love will be complete in us.

I John 4:12

I now address myself to the main theme of this paper which is the tentative contribution of a psychiatrist, using the discoveries of his subject to analyse a little deeper the mystery of love as encountered in man and in Christ. Scientists are not very fond of mysteries and the approach of psychology presents a particular challenge. The contributions of psychology and psychiatry have undoubtedly illuminated our understanding of love, yet it would be a gross exaggeration of the facts to pretend that such studies had exhausted either the complexity or the mystery of the experience we call love.

Nevertheless, the insights which are emerging both from dynamic psychology and other psychological approaches are of great interest to me for not only do they aid my understanding of human love but also prove to be instruments with which to explore the nature of divine love. There is a paradox here. The work of Freud and his successors, which has proved so much of a scandal to the Church in the last fifty years, is, when properly understood, an exciting and illuminating discipline which furthers our understanding of the nature of personal relationship mediated by affective bonds. 'Affect' is the term universally used to describe feelings and emotions; a substantial portion of psychology is concerned with the detailed intricacies of feelings and emotions in personal relations. A particular criticism of all psychoanalytic findings is that they are based on an examination of a few patients who were clearly abnormal and are, therefore, not applicable to humanity as a whole. Undoubtedly caution is required in drawing conclusions from the particular and generalising without further careful studies. On the other hand the study of an individual in great detail, as in psychoanalysis, allows great insight to be gained into the sequence of pathological events in the life of that individual.

Let me illustrate this point by considering three aspects of love; namely, separateness, freedom and the absence of fear. Human beings start life in a symbiotic state, in a nine months gestation period ending in a biological separation at birth. There follows a process covering nearly two decades of gradual separation between child and parent in which there is a progressive shift from dependence, from similarity and imitation to separateness and differentiation which culminates in the second half of the second decade in which the young man or woman enters into a phase of marked independence with sufficient acquisition of physical, intellectual and emotional growth to take the initiative in life in a way which allows him to separate from parents, find his or her own job or profession and enter into sexual relationships. They now possess a separate identity which can be freely offered or withheld in such new relationships.

It is well known that if growth has not taken place normally then this step of separation from parents cannot be accomplished. The person is not able to detach himself or herself from the emotional ties of dependent relationship and, to the extent that they do not possess themselves sufficiently as separate persons, they cannot enter into relationships of love. In extreme cases they cannot leave home at all and remain with the parents or parent substitutes. They are unable to offer themselves to others because emotionally they are still extensions of their parents, to whom they are emotionally bound. They can go so far from their basic attachment, father or mother, but they are not free to detach themselves and they have to return to the source of their security and reassurance for their survival.

This freedom is very different from the traditional understanding of freedom associated, for example, with the notion of sin in the catechism. In order to sin there was needed sinful matter, full knowledge and full consent. Full knowledge and full consent here and in so much of our thinking hitherto implies intellectual insight and rational freedom. Clearly these are important but they are insufficient for the freedom of human action. Freedom of human action also requires a separate identity. By identity here is meant a self awareness, consisting of a separate existence from parents which is sufficiently free from anxiety, guilt and parental standards to initiate freely personal relationships. Such freedom is not a matter of conscious willing, as is recurrently shown in psychiatric clinics. Many young men and women wish to leave home yet cannot do so. Freud's emphasis on the unconscious is crucial here. Our behaviour is not only mediated through our conscious self but also through the unconscious part of ourselves within which reside, amongst other things, experiences of fear, conflict and uncertainty; at times such things totally determine the outcome of our behaviour.

Separateness and freedom are intimately linked with absence of fear. The fear of our aloneness, the fear of initiative, the fear through lack of confidence in our own unaided resources, the fear of making mistakes, the fear of losing control, the fear of being incompetent; — all these fears inhibit movement towards others or, if there is movement, it is towards persons or environments which are in fact parent substitutes. In the last decade or so the changes in the Church have made us aware how much the authoritarian structure of the past acted as a refuge for personalities who moved from one dependent relationship, in which their lives were organised by parents, to another similar relationship in which the Church took over the role of the parental figure instructing them and freeing them from the responsibility of initiative. Similarly, in marriage such men and women choose spouses to whom they relate in this child-parent manner. Years later the marriage breaks up as the emotional dependence gives way to independent maturity which severs the mutual links and renders the spouse an irrelevant person in their life. Indeed, when people say they have fallen out of love with their spouse and in love with somebody else, very often they are expressing the changes within themselves which require different, at times radically different, emotional relationships in order to do justice to their personality. Similarly a high percentage of priests and nuns leaving the Church at the present time are men and women who found their way to these vocations not because they had a genuine calling but because the structure of the priesthood and of the religious life could contain this emotional dependence which, although totally unconscious, was their primary need. Because of a marked change in the atmosphere within the Church, coinciding for many with their own maturation out of such needs, such people find their old way of life totally irrelevant to their newly discovered identity.

Such men and women, married or celibate, entered into their vocations believing that they were in love with God and their neighbour. A few years later their husband or wife, their superior or their community become objects of anger, experienced as stifling, suffocating

5

intruders in their lives. Very often they lose touch with God and their faith. What is the explanation? In my view we cannot love unless we first truly possess ourselves in a way that we are aware of our separate identity and are free to offer it to another person; to offer it in such a manner that we do not lose our individuality and yet are able to unite with the other in love. To achieve this we need to possess an identity which gives us a sense of inner continuity and sameness, the capacity to remain the same person despite changing demands in relationships and circumstances. It is of the essence of human love to possess a separate, clearly delineated identity which is freely available to another person in a way that can become fused and detached in an unceasing sequence of closeness and separateness: a closeness which is not afraid to make available the whole of oneself socially, physically and emotionally to another person; a separateness which allows fusion to take place without losing oneself. Love requires mature acceptance, by which I mean the capacity to accept the needs of another person without needing to take over control of the other person's freedom as a condition for our availability. When these conditions do not exist, then in my view the true circumstances for love do not exist; instead the danger of mutual deceit and exploitation exists.

Of course my description is that of the ideal. The overwhelming majority of human relationships contain an admixture of love and exploitation, conscious and unconscious.

The intensity of love also depends on the degree to which two people possess themselves. In brief, I am suggesting that love demands a personal availability to another person the depth of which depends on the degree of self possession which is not lost in the encounter of fusion.

Such total independence which acknowledges total dependence without diminution of self is the model of love in the Trinity in which three persons make themselves totally available to each other in relationships of equality and complementarity without losing their separate identities. The nature of this relationship, as indeed the identity of the persons, is a mystery which we can only penetrate to the extent that the divine persons have chosen to reveal themselves. This revelation is in its most complete form in Jesus Christ and the second half of this paper is a brief outline of love, in terms of availability, comparing the availability of Christ and that of other human beings.

In the thesis I am presenting, love reflects the degree to which we possess precisely a unique identity and are free to offer it to another person in a way that gives the other person full access to ourselves without sustaining a personal loss in the process which damages our identity. In this analysis we have to examine the Scriptures for the evidence that our Lord possessed an identity which contained the constituents of precision, clarity, consistency and continuity. In human terms our identity

6

emerges as an expression of our physical characteristics given to us by our parents through our genetic inheritance and the environmental influences – largely parental – which establish the human bonds through which we recognize ourselves and others as beings worthy of acknowledgement, recognition, acceptance and love.

Christ's identity had a truly human source of influence, that of Mary and Joseph, and a divine one, his Father. Such a complex source of origin might have led to confusion, to what is currently called a crisis of identity. In fact none occurred and the episode of the Temple is one of the rare psychological gems in the Scriptures.

> Three days later they found him in the Temple, sitting among the doctors, listening to them and asking them questions; and all those who heard him were astounded at his intelligence and his replies. They were overcome when they saw him and his mother said to him – "My child, why have you done this to us? See how your father and I have been looking for you." "Why were you looking for me?" he replied, "Did you not know that I must be busy with my Father's affairs?" But they did not understand what he meant. He then went down with them and came to Nazareth and lived under their authority.
>
> Luke 2: 46-51

This incident can be used by those who wish to emphasize the intellectual side of Christ, as showing his early brilliance confounding the doctors in the Temple. It can be used by those who, obsessed with authority and obedience – particularly between parent and child, want to use this as a cautionary tale. But these interpretations pale when we see the psychological significance of the event. At the age of twelve, Christ had already reached a degree of self-awareness in which *he knew* his identity. There was no doubt about the primacy of his relationship with his heavenly Father. He was able to detach himself from Mary and Joseph without apparently any sense of anxiety and address himself to a task about which he had no doubt whatsoever. At this early stage he could survive alone without any fear, separate from his parents and do so knowing that he would cause them suffering, once again apparently without any sense of guilt. This episode clearly suggests that by this age Christ had internally separated himself from his human parents, without any fear, anxiety or guilt, and had done so without rejecting them. This is the essence of child-parent separation: the child separates himself from his parents, delineates his own separate identity and then offers it to man and God in separate relationships of love but without any trace of parental rejection. This transaction is one which dynamic psychology has examined it detail. In the many instances where this separation has not taken place satisfactorily the growing person may remain attached to one or other parent emotionally in a way that prevents him from totally giving himself to another human being. "A mum's boy" or "a daddy's girl" are the common phrases to denote the extreme, complex confusion of identity and emotional fixation which underlie much disturbance of personal and sexual relationships.

It seems to me that, although Christ rejoined his family and complied externally with the social requirements of the day, he had already — by the age of twelve — a clear sense of his own relationship with the Father, which was in no way confused with his earthly relationship, and this process took place without having to deny the reality of his mother's existence. Thus he avoided so many of the damaging possibilities in human growth in which a person either remains too attached to his mother or rebels vigorously against her and subsequently has a hostile attitude to all women. In such a situation love suffers because a man's closeness to a woman results in a mixture of hostility and anxiety that she will deny his independent value and existence. The same can occur in a girl-father relationship. Christ had a normal development in which he experienced closeness with his mother and father and yet could separate himself from them, having a separate identity and mission both of which remained enigmatic to them. Such was the degree of his secure self possession that he did not need to spend anxious hours speculating whether or not to explain the situation to his parents. In the fullness of time they would understand his mission. In the meantime he knew and possessed himself unequivocally.

This identity is reaffirmed visibly at his baptism and at the transfiguration and finds repeated expression in St. John's gospel.

'I am the light of the world;
anyone who follows me will not be walking in the dark;
he will have the light of life.'

At this the Pharisees said to him, 'You are testifying on your own behalf; your testimony is not valid.' Jesus replied:

'It is true that I am testifying on my own behalf, but my testimony is still valid,
because I know where I come from and where I am going.'

John 8: 12-14

Who except God can have such self knowledge at the age of thirty? If Christ was not God then these words are clearly those of a sincere but utterly deluded human being. Such a claim springs either from a paranoid delusion or from a unique and total possession of self, one

8

which neither time nor change can influence as it shares in the eternal continuity and sameness of the divine essence. This total and unflinching possession of self formed the basis of Christ's total availability to others. This, in my view, is the essence of love. In human terms such a secure possession of self implies trust, self control and the capacity to take the initiative to reach others.

Our Lord's sense of trust provides us with a wonderful key to the understanding of human relationships. The trust in his own judgement was supreme. He had received all from the Father and he would give it all to others. There is no uncertainty, no equivocation. He knew well those he wished to choose as his intimate friends and after the original choice there was no doubt, no experimentation, no withdrawal. Here is the model of trust in personal relationship in which continuity, reliability and predictability are present. For those who could receive his whole self, and even the apostles found this difficult, there was constancy. No expectations were aroused which remained unfulfilled. Everything which he offered of himself he was prepared to give.

In contrast human love suffers from the fluctuation of needs and availability. To the extent our needs change, so does our reaction to the people to whom we relate. Furthermore, we are only available to others to the limited extent that we know ourselves. Change in our knowledge of ourselves and of our needs makes us unreliable in our relationships and the person who appears to be all one day is nothing the next. In this way we arouse expectations in others which we cannot fulfil and if relationships are not reliable and predictable they deceive, though mostly without intention or deliberation. We deceive others because we are deceived ourselves.

Christ was reliable. He could be trusted to be available no matter what the personal cost.

'I am the good shepherd;
I know my own
and my own know me
just as the Father knows me
and I know the Father;
and I lay down my life for my sheep.'

John 10: 14-16

Human love, which can achieve such perfect trust of its motivation and powers of execution, shares and participates in a love that has no limits, makes no empty promises and can always be relied upon to be unconditionally available.

Love not only requires the freedom to give ourselves to others, it demands that we should be able to understand what the needs of others

9

are. Throughout the ages the material needs of others such as food, drink, shelter, clothes have been recognized and immortalized in our Lord's address on the last judgement.

'Come, you whom my Father has blessed, take for your heritage the kingdom prepared to you since the foundation of the world. For I was hungry and you gave me food; I was thirsty and you gave me drink; I was a stranger and you made me welcome; naked and you clothed me; sick and you visited me, in prison and you came to see me.'

Matthew 26: 34-7

There followed the astonishment of the accepted and the rejected. The obvious interpretation of this text is the wilful neglect of the needy, but in my view something of greater significance emerges here. Not only is it incumbent upon us to respond to the need of others but, even more important, we have an obligation to recognize the need of others. This is an aspect of the human personality designated by the term empathy. By sympathy we share each other's unpleasant experiences; through empathy we have the capacity to put ourselves, in technical language to project ourselves, into the inner world of another person, recognize their needs, yet remain separate and so available in a way that their need, their distress or their love, does not overwhelm us. The capacity to empathize is one of the crucial characteristics of human love for there is nothing more devastating than to be in urgent need and this to remain unrecognized by those close to us. There are lots of examples of Christ's empathy, a quality portrayed with stunning brevity in the Gospel of St. John. 'Christ could tell what a man had in him.' (John 2: 25) This capacity to identify correctly and identify with the inner needs of those close to us is essential in reaching others. Christ's empathy with the physical needs of his audience is exemplified in the miracle of the feeding of the five thousand and in the innumerable episodes of healing. Contemporary psychology has focused attention, however, on another facet of love. It is possible to reach out to others physically, by doing things for them, and it is in this field that so much of Christian endeavour has been channelled. But human beings need to be reached with our feelings. Feelings in ourselves and in others have to be recognized, given and received. To the extent that love is confined to physical and intellectual communication alone, it is a distortion of an authentic human experience. The fear and confusion about sexuality in the Christian ranks have at times almost paralysed our understanding with regard to our feelings. Too often have we feared that these would lead to immoral acts.

All feelings are initiated in the heavenly experience of oneness between the young infant and its mother in which the feelings of recognition, acceptance and tenderness are exchanged unconditionally through looks, caresses and words. These needs remain permanently in human beings and psychoanalysts work continuously with human beings who have never experienced these feelings adequately and are handicapped in innumerable ways either in expressing or receiving them. A good deal of marital breakdown reflects such problems in which the partners can neither recognize each other's needs nor make available the appropriate feelings. The Western tradition which has emphasized so much the intellectual side of man has been undoubtedly a distinct handicap, at times setting up dehumanizing standards for men and women.

Many examples of Christ's empathy could be selected but I have chosen the one in Luke which demonstrates a heterosexual encounter that is emotional, tactile and verbal.

'One of the Pharisees invited him to a meal. When he arrived at the Pharisee's house and took his place at table a woman came in, who had a bad name in the town. She had heard he was dining with the Pharisee and had brought with her an alabaster jar of ointment. She waited behind him at his feet, weeping and her tears fell on his feet and she wiped them away with her hair; then she covered his feet with kisses and anointed them with the ointment.'

The Pharisee was shocked; here in all probability was a prostitute touching and kissing his guest.

'Then he turned to the woman. "Simon", he said, "You see this woman? I came into your house and you poured no water over my feet, but she has poured out her tears over my feet and wiped them away with her hair. You gave me no kiss, but she has been covering my feet with kisses ever since I came in. You did not anoint my head with oil, but she has anointed my feet with ointment. For this reason I tell you that her sins, her many sins, must have been forgiven her, or she would not have shown such great love." But he said to the woman – 'Your faith has saved you; go in peace.'

Luke 7: 36-50

Here is a superb example of availability and empathy involving

11

human feelings and emotions. Up to now this woman's hands and her body were given to men whose impoverishment was that they could not have stable relationships with a woman. She shared their incapacity, for this is the heart of all prostitution, the incapacity of a man or woman to enjoy anything but transient contact, an inability either to offer or receive any enduring exchanges of love. Christ knew her desperate need to communicate, physically and emotionally, an authentic part of herself which would reach the source of all authenticity from which she could receive the strength to do justice to her feminity in the future and to find peace in the present. He, the author of all love, made himself available to her and reached her through his empathetic acknowledgement of her needs.

Human love also heals and strengthens this way by making ourselves available to others so that they can acquire for the first time authentic experiences in which they discover their capacity to give themselves physically and emotionally in a genuine exchange of love rather than one of mutual exploitation which is the mark of all prostitution.

Love requires human availability, augmented by empathy and completed by a non-judgemental openness to ourselves and to others. What is meant by non-judgemental openness? This is a subject which has especially engaged the attention of analysts.

Freud stressed one great shift in human development — namely that from pleasure to reality. Each one of us starts as a seething mass of physical and emotional needs which in our first few years of life have to be satisfied with minimum frustration. As we grow older we can tolerate frustration increasingly and learn how to postpone our immediate needs, to defer gratification. This is the process which Freud designated as responding to reality. What happens, however, if our continual needs are not first organized and ordered in an increasingly mature way, but denied? What happens to the child who needs attention, physical closeness, expressions of affection and tenderness but cannot have them either because the parents are not available or because they actually reject their child or because its needs are in excess of the parental capacity to match them? If the need for love is overwhelming and yet cannot be satisfied, very often the way to deal with such an impossible situation is to endow the particular need with feelings of shame and guilt or to repress it, to render it unconscious. In one way or another there is a part of oneself which becomes split off, condemned and rejected. These parts of ourselves have been called complexes by analysts and tend to make up the vulnerable bits of ourselves which can only be handled by various continuous patterns called defences. These defences include the process of denial, in which some painful and vital part of ourselves is denied; rationalisation in which the true motives, usually emotional ones, are substituted by some other explanation; or projection in which impulses, wishes and feelings, both positive and negative, are experienced as being located in others. These and other mechanisms protect us from experiencing needy or unpleasant parts of others. To the extent we are isolated from such feelings within ourselves we are incapable of recognizing their presence or validity in others or responding to these feelings when they are offered to us by others. The freedom to enjoy sexual experiences is condemned as immoral because these are unavailable or forbidden in ourselves, the capacity to take the initiative in expressing feelings is condemned as showing lack of self control; the appreciated controlling man may, in fact, have to exercise such a tight hold over his angry feelings otherwise he may let loose havoc with his destructiveness. Envy is not only a matter of lusting after our neighbour's wife or goods, it may be the expression of a condemned or unavailable part of our inner world which is freely accepted, experienced and appreciated in another person.

The Jews found themselves precisely in this situation with Christ. They could not receive his total acceptance of himself.

> The Jews fetched stones to stone him so Jesus said to them; 'I have done many good works for you to see, works from my Father; for which of these are you stoning me?' The Jews answered him; 'We are not stoning you for doing a good work but for blasphemy: you are only a man and you claim to be God.'
>
> John 10: 31-3

The Jews condemned him because they could not accept his claim of being one with the Father. Christ never wavered or compromised in this claim. He could not judge, condemn or, in equivalent psychological language, reject or deny one iota of himself. To the extent he could accept himself unconditionally as a fully human and divine form he was able to accept others. There was no part of himself from which he was cut off and there was no person or part of a person he needed to reject through failure to comprehend their humanity or need. He was totally open to himself and to others. Human beings fall far short of such acceptance of themselves, let alone of others, and psychoanalysis has proved a complicated but unique way of reaching those portions of ourselves which were locked out of our awareness or capacity to experience and allowing the reintegration of these split off parts of ourselves. To the extent we accept these in ourselves without condemnation we become more fully human and accept others without judgement or condemnation.

This is not to say that from time to time we shall not misuse the

13

gifts of God in ourselves or offend and hurt others with our aggression. Forgiveness and reparation are essential for safeguarding love. We have to forgive ourselves repeatedly without losing our own value as people capable of loving. We have to seek forgiveness from others without losing our innate capacity to love. We have to forgive others without humiliating them or rejecting their renewed endeavours to reach us. Human love often stumbles and falls at this point because we find it difficult to forgive ourselves or others. In these situations our angry rejection of ourselves and others is greater than our loving acceptance.

Thus non-judgemental openness as used in this paper includes the traditional concept of humility but goes beyond this to the fundamental notion that we cannot love others unless first we have lovingly accepted and acknowledged ourselves without condemnation. If we do not judge ourselves, we will not judge others; if we do not reject ourselves, we will have little need to reject others. It is of the utmost significance that, although Christ was very severe on the Jews in certain aspects of their behaviour, there is no evidence anywhere that he rejected a single human being who wished, however dimly, to respond to him and such was his availability that he could respond to the slightest intimation. Indeed the slimmest initiative as shown by the apostles was enlarged and converted to unlimited depths of donation.

The theme of this paper has developed in a way so that love has been equated with availability in human relationships. It is a fitting concept for a liturgical conference. For it is in the mass that we find the exact equivalent of the two. In the farewell discourse in the Gospel of St. John we find these words:-

My little children,
I shall not be with you much longer,
You will look for me, and, as I told the Jews,
Where I am going you cannot come.
I give you a new commandment: love one another;
Just as I have loved you,
You also must love one another.
By this love you have for one another,
Everyone will know that you are my disciples.'

John 13: 33-5

Shortly after this Jesus took some bread, broke it, gave it to his disciples and said — 'Take it and eat, this is my body.' Then he took the cup, gave thanks and gave it to them. 'Drink all of you from this, for this is my blood, the blood of the covenant, which is to be poured out for many for the forgiveness of sins.'

Here we find total and complete availability in which God offers himself to each one of us and which our Catholic tradition retains in the solemn sacrifice of the mass. Human love cannot imitate such complete giving but in all human relationships between man and man, man and woman, this is the model to which it aspires.

PART I

The following three essays were written to meet different needs. The first was an article in 'The Way' while the next two formed part of the annual conference for superiors held at Spode House, Rugeley, in 1971. Although the Spode lectures naturally took account of the special needs of those present their general principles are applicable to those outside the religious life. All three essays develop the concepts of self-acceptance, the realization of one's potential through positive reinforcement, and the importance of feelings.

WHAT IS SENSITIVITY?

Spirit is a difficult word to describe or to define. The Greek word *pneuma,* meaning breath or wind, came to be used for the 'breath of life'. But it was another Greek word, *nous,* which had a more decisive influence and development. It came to mean successively the active principle of order in all things: in Plato, the faculty which allows man to contemplate the changeless eternal world of forms; in Aristotle, the activity which is characteristic of man. For St Augustine, and the Christian tradition it came to mean more than the Greek just described; it became dynamic contact between man and God. In this sense the human spirit is the encounter between the finite and the infinite, the limited and the absolute, the temporal and the eternal.

The spirit operates in the whole person; it has been further delineated by the activities of intellect and will or knowledge and love. The philosopher is concerned to elucidate in greater detail the components of these factors in terms of logic, definition and meaning. The academic psychologist concerned with the study of personality will also consider his discipline fit to examine the cognitive and conative aspects of human functioning.

In this essay emphasis will be placed on some aspects of the emotional development of the personality and on the place of feelings – the aspects of human behaviour always recognized but so often thrust into the background by the enormous importance attached to the reasoning faculties of man.

Feelings and emotions are complex phenomena, subject to many theoretical formulations with no clear-cut answers. For the student interested in the academic aspects M.B. Arnold's *The Nature of Emotion* will give a guide to recent work.

In this paper the dynamic aspects of feelings and emotions will be considered as they are seen in ordinary human development.

Work in the last decade by psychoanalysts who have left orthodox Freudian psychology far behind, tends to stress, as some of the early dissenters did, man's potentiality for growth treated as an entity capable of realization at critical periods of his development as a child, in a complementarity between the child's needs and the appropriate parental response. The well-known American psychologist, H.E. Erikson, has built up one of the most comprehensive systems of this type of thinking.

Erikson considers that basic feelings emerge in the child at certain critical periods and need the corresponding nurturing by the parents to develop them fully.

The first year of life is critical for our survival. According to Erikson, in this first year we acquire a sense of trust. It is clear from his writings that this sense of trust does not cease to develop after the first year: it is an unfolding process which continues once its foundations have been laid. The opposite is that of mistrust.

When we consider life at all stages, the importance of the feeling of trust stands out as of primary importance and the trust which springs from this experience is the indispensable requirement for all future relationships in which friendship and love are exchanged. The relationship between trust and faith is of interest both to theology and psychology. Erikson himself has this to say:

It is not the psychologist's job to decide whether religion should or should not be confessed and practised in particular words and rituals. Rather the psychological observer must ask whether or not in any area under observation religion and tradition are living psychological forces creating the kind of faith and conviction which permeates a parent's personality and thus reinforces the child's basic trust in the world's trustworthiness. The psychopathologist cannot avoid observing that there are millions of people who cannot really afford to be without religion and whose pride in not having it is that much whistling in the dark. On the other hand, there are millions who seem to derive faith from other than religious dogmas, that is, from fellowship, productive work, social action, scientific pursuit and artistic creation. And again, there are millions who profess faith yet in practice mistrust both life and man. With all of these in mind it is worth-while to speculate on the fact that religion through the centuries has served to restore a sense of trust at regular intervals in the form of faith while giving tangible form to a sense of evil which it promises to ban. *Psychological Issues,* Vol. I.

Erikson's speculations deserve serious consideration whatever their ultimate validity. What is not in doubt is the fact that faith, man's response to God, either directly or through our neighbour, requires the quality of trust which is a feeling engendered in the earliest period of life. God is reached through our parents, not only in the traditional sense of agents who teach us the rudiments of faith but as the living springs providing us with the prototypes of the meaning of God, the source of infinite trust. The trust we receive from our parents gives us also trust in ourselves, the basis of self-possession and acceptance.

To the second and third year, Erikson gives the feeling of autonomy, accompanied by its opposites, shame and doubt. These are the years in which the child acquires an extensive range of new skills: talking, walking, feeding itself, dressing, handling a whole new range of objects and learning the rudiments of socialization. All this provides a unique and rapid extension of effective expression of its humanity. This is of course not learned at once; it is acquired through a process of trial and error in which the parent provides an umbrella-like support and security, giving encouragement, ready to step in and clear up the mess or give a helping hand. The child thus acquires *self-control without loss of self-esteem.* This is a formula which remains basic to human beings throughout their lives; it is at the very heart of the renewal of Christianity at the present moment. The Church is not called Mother as an accident of history. The Christian community, the Church, is the nurturing source of our faith, and needs to act like the human mother, positively, enabling maximum growth in each baptized member, encouraging a truly independent, self-reliant, self-realizing personality. The agonizing conflicts within the Church are to be found precisely in the gap between man's possibilities to develop his potential in the secular world without an equivalent opportunity or freedom to relate to God in an appropriate spiritual manner. Instead, the emphasis has been placed on man's ineptitude, limitations, and need to rely on the strength of mother for survival; all of which inculcated a sense of impotence and unnecessary dependence.

While the second and third years are principally concerned with the acquisition of autonomy — the ability to function in essentials without external support, the next two or three years usher in the sense of initiative. Locomotion extends well beyond the immediate confines of home, reaching the neighbourhood, the kindergarten classes and beyond. Language is now perfected and imaginative initiative is the catalyst for all the new horizons that open. Having discovered in the previous phase that he is a person, the child now wants to find out what kind of person he is going to be. The result will depend a great deal on the encouragement and support that is given by parents and teachers.

Certain feelings run counter to autonomy and initiative, not only in childhood when these patterns of behaviour are first established but throughout life when they repeat themselves. Mention has already been made of the feeling of shame which may accompany the trial and error method of learning new skills. This sense of embarrassment does not cease in childhood, as all adults know when they are confronted with a new situation such as changing the wheel of a car, ordering a meal in a foreign restaurant, learning to drive a car, passing an examination in a new subject, making a public speech for the first time, and so on.

Initiative is coupled by Erikson with a sense of guilt; and this universal feeling needs further detailed understanding. Traditional spiritual formulations placed the sense of guilt at a later stage in the development of the child: that is, with the so-called 'advent of the use of reason' at seven or eight. Such a conceptualization depended heavily on an understanding of the personality entirely in terms of intellect, reason and will. When the child was capable of understanding, differentiating, and acting purposively in the choice between right and wrong, then it could experience a sense of righteousness or guilt — depending on its choice. This view is no longer adequate to explain feelings of guilt and shame for the simple reason that these feelings are established in the first half-dozen years in terms of inter-personal exchanges between the child and its parents which have nothing to do with reason. These feelings are aroused as a result of pleasing and displeasing parents, closeness and alienation from the source of all love. They precede any guilt which arises from conscious and deliberate violations of objective reality. Thus there are two 'feeling-systems' operating within all personalities. One refers to approval and disapproval in personal terms, exchanging positive or negative feelings with those who matter to us; the other is based on experiences relating to the acceptance or violation of impersonal laws, civil or ecclesiastical.

This division is vital for our spiritual life. Our relationship with God is a personal encounter, in which feelings of personal significance are of the same quality as those experienced in childhood. Spiritual life has been based, in recent centuries, on the obedience to laws which have emphasized a strictly legal framework of reference. This emphasis on law diminished the infinitely more important personal core of loving encounter between us and God, which is a continuation of the intimate ties between child and parent. To this, Christian spirituality is now returning, by placing love at the centre of the man-man and man-God experience, and law at the periphery, which corresponds exactly to the growth of the human personality.

Self-esteem is of such importance in Christian spirituality that it needs further amplification. All of us are born in a state of helplessness and depend totally on our parents for survival. We survive because they nurture us, we learn to love others because we have first felt loved by them; we acquire our sense of significance, of feeling wanted and appreciated, through these distinctive attributes which we receive from them. In a wider sense it can be seen that all this is possible because God first loved us, the meaning of justification by faith. But let us return to the child-parent relationship. What happens if, for one reason or another, the child does not experience these feelings of being wanted and loved by its parents? In the circumstances in which it finds itself, it is too small and helpless to risk blaming them for their failure. The situation is in fact reversed: the child blames itself or accepts the parental accusation of its own badness and unworthiness as real. From

21

now on, whenever its legitimate needs for attention and love are experienced, the child will feel greedy, demanding, selfish and self-centred. These feelings will be reinforced later on theologically by a false spirituality which, lacking the understanding of true humility, will compound the problems of such people by translating legitimate but unfulfilled yearning into 'selfish demands'.

A situation is now reached where the parents, and parental figures such as God, will be treated in an idealized way. They and they alone are good, strong, powerful and rich; by comparison the child is small, insignificant and unworthy of attention. This is a familiar picture; and such people who on the surface appear to exhibit the appropriate characteristics of obedience, submission, humility and self-denial, are full of anger, resentment and envy, not only because their legitimate needs were not met in childhood but because they live emotionally in a state which reinforces this denial. Having never received adequately the tokens of acceptance, they have grown up with an acute sense of their unworthiness which now does not deserve love and acceptance. Psychoanalysis has penetrated this tangle of twisted layers of the human personality by uncovering the basic distortions. When the fundamental denial of the appropriate feeling is reached, such a person also reaches his anger and fury at feeling cheated and denied. This is the moment when many people, unless they have recourse to psychoanalysis or equivalent help, lose their faith. The loss is difficult to interpret because, until then, they appeared to fulfil all the correct external criteria; yet underneath there was no real contact of love between themselves and God. On the contrary there was fear, submission and self-rejection, with exaggerated emphasis on personal insignificance and unworthiness. All this has nothing to do with an authentic relationship with God: he does not seek our meiosis or diminution, but the greatest possible realization of his image in us which he has freely bestowed in an act of love.

To the extent that the institutional Church has been seen and experienced as a depriving mother, scornful of man's legitimate achievements scientifically, sociologically and psychologically, there has been a corresponding angry withdrawal from and abandonment of Mother Church, experienced as a parental figure incapable of loving her children appropriately and letting them grow up effectively. Both the mother and the children are feeling hurt. The mother because her overprotection was not recognized by her to have been a stunting denial of her children's humanity; the sons and daughters because their act of rebellion has left them cut off from their authentic source of love and attachment. The *rapprochement* is slow and painful, but it has to go on.

One way that psychology can contribute to this in the field of sensitivity is by reassessing the meaning of humility. There can be no true humility in the absence of a core of self-acceptance. This self-acceptance enables people to feel worthy of attention, praise and acknowledgement in accordance with their gifts; but also, and this is far more important, on the basis that they are worthy to be loved simply as persons and independent of their talents.

We cannot earn or buy love from others; we can only receive it and accept it on the basis that, having first been loved by our parents for simply being ourselves, we continue to be loved by others on the same basis. In the same way we love others freely for what they are rather than for what they do. A false sense of humility which tries to reinforce a basic and unconscious feeling of being unlovable has no place in a sensitive structure of spirituality — one that always seeks to discover the basic goodness present in our very existence, enhanced by the grace which God has freely given to us in baptism. Those who are loaded with a sense of their own inadequacy and use humility as a means of reinforcing their own rejection of themselves, need to be encouraged to abandon this 'false self' and to be reached afresh on the basis of unconditional love and acceptance.

Jealousy is a different process, basically related to the anxiety of losing something good through the intervention of a third person. Envy belongs to a one-to-one relationship, jealousy characteristically to a triangular situation. The young child is threatened by the arrival of younger brothers and sisters, by the presence of the father who wants the attention of mother, by other children who are potential predators of his goods, status and significance. Jealousy and competition have to be separated; and once again the answer lies in the core of self-esteem. All those who are basically secure within themselves about their own fundamental value and goodness because they have felt sufficiently loved are capable of distinguishing between the outcome of a competitive situation, in which the best person wins without destroying the significance of the losers, and jealousy, in which the success of others threatens a personal eclipse. Such personal calamity is likely to occur when the individual who is lacking in sufficient self-esteem needs the visible proof of success and total defeat of others as the only evidence for his or her own value, now gained through activity rather than a reassurance received through personal interaction with others. Other people are hell, according to Sartre; but this is true only if there is no abiding heaven within oneself, however small, given once and for all by parents and through them by God which no-one can take away.

Erikson finds faith and trust intimately linked, introduced in the first year of life. The next few years allow the growth of autonomy and initiative. If parents approve and encourage these tentative but gradually more confident acts of achievement, then to faith is added hope, laying the foundations of expectation, fulfilment and achievement which, according to Erikson, develop a little later on.

If, for one reason or another, parents cannot allow this show of independent realization, then a sense of gradual uselessness and despair will take the place of hope. The despair is experienced in two ways. It is a despair interpreted as a personal rejection. Nothing is ever done well enough to please or satisfy the parents; and, by inference, the child never feels personally acceptable whatever its concrete achievements. Then, later on, it is confirmed in its own sense of uselessness both in activity and through this in personal significance. Such inadequacy is usually rationalized in feelings of badness experienced as selfishness, self-centredness or egocentricity. But this despair goes deeper than the surface expression of failure. Ultimately, it is linked with the sense of having the temerity to challenge the monopoly of success encountered in grown-ups. The right to succeed belongs to parents, figures of authority, everyone who knows and understands more, to anyone, that is, except themselves. They admire and respect others, whilst at the same time expressing their envy by inviting them to become humble like themselves. They are happiest co-existing with others whose failures and defects appear to make them bed-fellows. This attitude lies at the root of the sudden and unexpected viciousness which is expressed when a person of authority falls from grace in one way or another.

Contemporary man is once again at cross-purposes with a traditional interpretation of Christianity which sees the God-man relationship in an over-submissive hierarchical structure, where each one has his place and no one can move one rung up the ladder without permission. Modern man has in fact said: 'I can do without God, or if necessary I shall be God-like'. He has rejected Christianity which appears forbidding, embarrassing and humiliating. Such a view of Christianity has no scriptural foundation. God created man in his image and invites him constantly to participate in the fulness of love which God himself is. Man does not need to compete with God because the Father sent his Son in whom we are all one. There is no show of strength in the Creator, only an abundance of love which he wants us to respond to and to share with him.

> On that day
> You will understand that I am in my Father
> and you in me and I in you.
>
> John 14: 20

The confidence which we receive from our parents, that we matter to them independently of our works and achievements, is reinforced in our whole spiritual life, which confirms that we matter to God: because we exist and are offered constantly a relationship of significance, independently of our worthiness. But if our parents have given us the basis for loving ourselves, we have also to love others, since Christianity is based on the commandment of loving our neighbour as ourselves.

So far this essay has been deliberately concerned with the second half of that commandment, the 'as ourselves', thus reversing the traditional order. The reason for this is simply that we cannot love others unless we first know the meaning of loving our own selves. All loving of others which is not founded on self-acceptance is a precarious exercise, because underneath we need others more than they need us; and sooner or later our need will come through. Very often it is explicitly clear on the surface in all those whose loving is based entirely on the condition of being appreciated and acknowledged in return, and ceases immediately this need is not fulfilled. But granted that we have a minimal acceptance of ourselves, how do we love others?

We cannot love others unless we are able to recognize their needs. In man's history these needs have been predominantly material. Food, shelter, warmth, the cure of disease, poverty, are self-evident requirements to which human beings have responded and which the Church has made prominent in its caring. But as these needs recede in the West with the intervention of the State, at least for large numbers of the community, we are recognizing far more clearly a different sort of hunger: the yearning of human beings who, being strangers to themselves and to others through their emotional isolation and impoverishment, are anxious to rediscover the meaning of life in personal terms. But this yearning of society reflects accurately the meaning of Christianity, if only the latter can find the right language and understanding to reach the hungry and lost sheep of this age.

In order to recognize and meet this quest in others, what is needed is the capacity to 'empathize'. Sympathy is the ability to feel for others; empathy, on the other hand, enables us to feel with others, to put ourselves in their shoes without losing our own separate existence. So often loving never starts because the emotional requirements of others are not recognized; or it stops too soon because, having recognized the needs of others, the giver becomes afraid of being swallowed up in their demands. Empathy allows an identification of the emotional predicament of others. It is beautifully and succinctly described in Christ in St John's gospel:

But Jesus knew them all and did not trust himself to them; He never needed evidence about any man; he could tell what a man had in him.

John 2: 25

To tell what another human being is thinking and feeling requires unerring insight, and our Lord had just that. His empathy extended beyond intellectual comprehension. He felt the inner world of others, and was ready and able to do this because there was no part of himself with which he was not familiar and which had not been accepted by him. Since he did not need to reject any part of himself, he could reach and be reached without having to withdraw or hold himself back.

Such empathy coincided with an unlimited availability, which is another characteristic in the process of loving. This availability is not merely physical presence but, even more important, the quality of the exchange. Much has been learned from the psychological sciences and the process of psychoanalysis and psychotherapy. In fact, what this availability means is the offering to another person of a second chance to grow up emotionally. The process of growing up is complicated. We need others to help us to see ourselves, to reach those bits of ourselves which are unconscious or have never developed. Having been assisted in this way, we still need them for a period in an exchange in which we learn new ways of feeling and reacting. It is not enough to understand intellectually the nature of a problem, we have to learn step by step new patterns of emotional behaviour; and for this we need the help, encouragement and support of others who love us as they need us to love them.

This availability avoids judging and giving advice. The judging is already taking place in the other person who is evaluating his own inner world and chooses to change. If we judge others, we are merely reinforcing their own sense of guilt and alienation. Since they are already in the midst of these feelings, our own reproach will yield little of value. This approach runs counter to the traditional belief that we have to stir up in people a sense of their own badness. They, more than anyone else, know their imperfections, what they need from us is the availability of patience and concern, which will provide a fresh opportunity to learn new ways of interacting. Those who do not feel the need for change will receive the criticism of others with indifference, pay the price demanded by the law or morality, but remain untouched in the core of their personality.

Similarly regarding advice: a true change of heart must be a free action of every person. People cannot run their lives our way, through our advice. They are certainly going to ask for it; but far more important is to help them to reflect on their own inner world, from which will emerge the points that need strengthening or changing.

Empathy and non-judgmental availability are in fact the foundations on which psychoanalysis, psychotherapy and counselling are based. It is taking an exceedingly long time for Christianity to discover that, in these processes instituted by an atheist, some of the most authentic aspects of Christ's relationships with others will be found.

Instead the therapist, and that means all of us who act as therapists to others as they do to us, concentrates on an entirely new dimension, that of feeling. Feelings of trust, mistrust, hope, despair, initiative, achievement, envy, jealousy and self-esteem have all been mentioned.

Many find feelings difficult to experience or to share with others. They cut off into a physical or intellectual way of experiencing themselves and others. Hysterical behaviour is the technical term for describing the transformation of feelings into bodily substitutes, and the whole of psychosomatic medicine examines this aspect of human behaviour. Rationalization is the commonest attribute, the particular attribute of the West, which has placed such an enormous emphasis on reason and intellect. One wonders if Christ would have been remembered to-day if his divinity had been proclaimed in purely metaphysical terms. Sensitivity is that aspect of the personality which allows us to reach and be reached in affectionate terms, whether of joy or sadness, anxiety or trust, hope or despair.

But what is the purpose of sensitivity? The whole message of Christianity is to be found in the conviction that God exists, that he has revealed himself, and that his nature is love. Furthermore he has created us in his image and invited us to love ourselves and others as he loves himself and us. Faith sustains us in striving for this goal; and as our knowledge of human beings deepens we learn in greater depth the meaning of being human. We are now reaching the stage of confronting the layer of being which goes beyond intellect and reason, touching the instinctual, affectionate parts of man. Man's response to himself, to his fellow human beings and above all to God, has to incorporate this level of awareness which adds a whole new dimension of sensitivity, allowing us to realize a little more the image of God in us.

INTEGRITY AND PERSON I

The Jews said — "Now we know for certain that you are possessed. Abraham is dead, and the prophets are dead and yet you say, 'Whoever keeps My word will never know the taste of death.' Are you greater than our father Abraham who is dead? The prophets are dead, too. Who are you claiming to be?" Jesus answered:

> "If I were to seek my own glory,
> that would be no glory at all;
> my glory is conferred by the Father,
> by the one of whom you say 'He is our God'
> Although you do not know Him;
> But I know Him
> And if I were to say: I do not know Him
> I should be a liar as you are
> liars yourselves.
> But I do know Him and I faithfully
> keep His word.
> Your father Abraham rejoiced
> to think that he would see My Day;
> he saw it and was glad."

The Jews then said — "You are not fifty yet and you have seen Abraham!" Jesus replied:

> "I tell you most solemnly
> before Abraham ever was
> I am."

At this they picked up stones to throw at Him, but Jesus hid Himself and left the Temple.

John 8: 52-59

We can sympathise with the Jewish spectators in the Temple. Christ was trying to tell them who he was and the vastness of His claim was proving too much for them. I wonder constantly when reading the gospels how I would have reacted to the challenge that Christ was offering to his fellow men and women. He was claiming to have existed

28

before and through time and such an utterance could have come either from a person whose mind was deranged or from the only one who could make such a declaration without violating integrity, namely God himself.

The Jews, or most of them, reacted by picking up stones to throw at him, but what would our reaction have been? Fortunately we are not asked to answer this impossible question. But we have to respond to Christ in each and every neighbour we relate to. Even more important we have to try to understand ourselves as fully as possible in order to approach the integrity with which Christ related to the world around him. One thing can be claimed with confidence. If Christ's integrity did not survive the perpetual questioning that his presence must have aroused, it is certain that there would have been no apostles and no followers. His expectations of himself and of others could not have been sustained without the sort of evidence that must have amply reinforced his claims to authenticity. Similarly in our lives we need authenticity. Any discoveries that others may make of our deceptions, willed or accidental, pale into insignificance compared with the need for consistency in our own image of ourselves.

These two essays are not going to be concerned with metaphysical or philosophical description of what is meant by person. They will attempt to describe in psychological terms the experiences of people in relation to themselves and to others.

Being and Body

Our Lord was able to surprise and confound his listeners by his unequivocal attestation of existence.

> "I tell you most solemnly
> before Abraham ever was
> I am."

Christ has a clear awareness of himself which transcended time and place. His answer was more than an imaginative reply to an embarrassing situation. He believed utterly in the truth of his statement. His integrity was vested in the veracity of his reply. Our life has smaller dimensions of width and depth but our reality, who we are, requires integrity just as much as that of Christ.

The sources of our own information about ourselves are grounded first of all in our physical reality. Height, weight, colour, shape, movement, sound, wellbeing, ill health are the constant transmitters of information which guide us. Sensation and perception such as sound, vision, touch, temperature, depth, intensity in various combinations sharpen our physical awareness of ourselves. Sigmund Freud went as far as to say that our personality depends on two basic instincts, sexuality and aggression. Certainly both of these experiences are intensely physical and to them could be added our elementary physical needs such as those for food, air, water and avoidance of extremes of temperature.

You will note that I used the word "need" to introduce these characteristics. It is painfully clear that we need food, water, etc., to survive but Christianity has been slow to appreciate the equivalent significance of sexuality and aggression with the result that these elements in our personality have been severely underrated.

These physical sensations, coupled with the physiological rhythm of rest and energy expenditure, sleep and wakefulness, the menstrual and reproductive cycles and others provide us with a vital sense of our being constantly modified by age.

Being and Intellect

One specific attribute of the human being, a vital part which separates man from animals, is focused on his use of reason. We do not use our bodies in a vacuum. We are governed by reason, logic and will. Intellect and will have played an enormous part in Western philosophy and inevitably in Christian thought. A person is commonly judged by the quality of his intellect which is considered his most vital means of expression. Hence the emphasis on education which shapes our intellectual abilities for thought and action. We tend to describe people in terms of their capacity to think, to imagine, to be logical or creative and to act consistently with the dictates of what is reasonable.

Such is the importance we attach to our minds that much of our assessment of ourselves and others is laden with intellectual measures which are considered to be a vital indicator of personal worth. In a society increasingly conscious of qualifications, those who do not possess these are conscious of an acute impoverishment. This shift of emphasis has been clearly felt in religious life, particularly in those congregations which make a sharp differentiation between the academically qualified and the rest.

Realisation of Potential

This experience, familiar to all of us in one way or another, singles out an aspect of being which is increasingly holding our attention, namely the realisation of our potential. Let us return to our Lord. He insists that he knows the Father and if he were to deny this he would be a liar. If he were to deny the fullness of his being he would be betraying his own integrity.

All of us have a similar duty to realise fully our potential to become as perfect as our heavenly Father. In fact this means examining the limits of which we are capable of growing physically and intellectually.

There are, of course, limitations imposed by human nature in general and by our own individual potential in particular. This is what is known technically as our innate endowment which reflects the genetic and constitutional make-up of each one of us. This is the part we have inherited from our parents and any additional changes which occur in the course of reproduction. What we have received is further influenced by the quality of our environment. The environment reflects the material, intellectual and social atmosphere which aids or hinders the realisation of our talents. Scientists argue unceasingly about how much of our personality is the result of nature and how much of nurture. The details do not concern us, but what is beyond argument is the fact that the quality of the environment does undoubtedly influence the enhancement or retardation of our potential.

Thus a vital contribution to any understanding of integrity is the personal need to ensure that we live in an environment which is as conducive to our growth as possible. In childhood this is a task primarily assigned to our parents but one of the real changes in recent history is the increasing freedom of children to have a say regarding their own lives. Up to a short time ago this was considered impertinent and wrong. Authority knew best whether it was parents, teachers, rulers or those wielding authority in the Church. Today we look at this differently. Clearly there must be authority or societies will plunge into chaos. But order has no meaning as an end in itself. It exists to foster the welfare of the community and one vital aspect of this is ensuring the uninterrupted and maintained growth of individuals. Balance has to be preserved, of course, so that one person's growth does not diminish another's. But this principle is no excuse for adopting the minimum level of advance for the community as a whole.

All these issues engage our attention vitally in religious life today when men and women are leaving unexpectedly and there is a shortage of new vocations. My experience with scores of such people has indicated to me beyond any shadow of doubt that, however diverse the reasons offered, frequently at the heart of the matter is the feeling of the individuals that their integrity in terms of growth and realisation of their potential is threatened vitally. Sometimes this can be put clearly into words, sometimes it leads to an inexplicable tension and frustration which expresses itself in symptoms of depression, anxiety, restlessness and acute unhappiness. Often the distress of the situation is compounded in several ways; e.g. by the community which, without comprehending the dilemma of the individual, labels his action in terms of failure to be generous, loving or self-sacrificing enough for Christ or more negatively as being selfish, too independent, too worldly, etc. The individual concerned knows that his environment is inimical to his growth but finds it difficult to identify correctly what are the issues and feels anxious, torn between his loyalty to God and to himself.

In these situations the concepts of growth, realisation of potential and integrity can provide invaluable means to understanding the situation. There are certain questions that can be asked even if they cannot be easily answered. Is this person trained adequately? Is the training which he has received in the past suitable for the present? Is the work he is doing in tune with his own wishes? Are his wishes capable of being realised without physical and intellectual strain? Is he receiving enough active encouragement and support in achieving the work he has been ordered to do? Is enough attention being paid to the changes that occur in all of us throughout the years? Has enough variety been offered? Is the person really in tune with his hopes and aspirations? Above all, if there is a conflict between the needs of the community and that of the individual, has this been perfectly understood by all so that the sacrifice made by the person is recognised and terminated at the first possible point? We will return to this in the second paper when we consider the psychological apects of integrity.

Social Aspects

You may well consider that all these questions are routine evaluations that go on continuously in all communities. Perhaps the ones I have dealings with are the exception but often I see a lack of awareness which is destroying a vocation unnecessarily. The focus of the tension is often expressed in terms of justice, freedom and equality, and since these are the social characteristics which govern the life of any community, they need careful attention. Some of the most obvious tensions surround the issue of freedom which needs a detailed examination. I am personally concerned that many religious leave and few enter because of the conviction that they will not be free to be themselves in religious life. Freedom has thus become a keynote of personal integrity.

No one questions the importance of freedom as an inalienable human right. Each generation has to ask afresh what kind of freedom it is to accept and how it is to be expressed. Here the Catholic Church and the religious life are particularly handicapped because, although we paid lip service to personal freedom in the past, we acted on different principles. These were authoritarian, hierarchical principles in which obedience, blind obedience at that, was overvalued. In the space of a few years there has been a remarkable change. Part of our difficulty is that the change has been too rapid, producing extreme reactions. There are those who wish to push the limits of personal freedom to extremes unacceptable to the majority. There are others who find any change so painful that while they pay lip service to it they do not allow it to alter the substance of their lives.

Let us examine some familiar elements in this controversial picture.

A feature with which we are so familiar is the conviction in the past that the superior stood in the place of God in some mysterious way and his or her decisions were ultimately the best for the individual.

We know now that such a view of the relationship between superior and community is incorrect and that much damage resulted from it. In the reconstruction of religious life new regulations have brought about a more balanced situation. But an extreme reaction to the past is the conclusion that superiors are now incapable of ever reaching the correct decision for anyone. This is equally manifestly absurd. Freedom in this situation seems to me to be far more pertinent with respect to the mode of dialogue between those in charge and others. With the demise of the authoritarian system and the absence of stigma attached to withdrawal from religious life, there now exists a far more genuine situation in which freedom can be exercised. Superiors now know that if they do not meet effectively the needs of their community, all those who are capable of leaving will do so because the restraints are so markedly less. Fear no longer operates in either direction. Superiors are no longer forced to accept candidates merely to replenish the ranks of the community. The emphasis on the maturity of candidates will gradually ensure that religious life will shift its concern from sheer numbers to quality. This is a change which can be welcomed unequivocally and will allow a much greater freedom of exchange between religious and their superiors. Neither party will be primarily motivated by subtle social pressures which really do curtail genuine freedom. Both parties will be able to express their needs far more freely.

Just at this moment of transition this can produce genuine difficulties. Those who have been in religious life for a long time find the greater freedom difficult to grasp and are pained and shocked when the younger generation expresses itself in ways which would have been unimaginable a few years ago. Some expressions of freedom can produce violent clashes. Dress, freedom of movement, drinking, social activities such as visiting theatres, cinemas, concerts, the manner of recreation within the community, personal friendships and expressions of affection, privacy versus communion, all these and many others are closely connected with personal freedom.

One of the standard replies from those in authority who are out of tune with the changes is − "We have our rules to which we have to adhere". This is certainly true, but the real question that has to be asked is not whether an individual is breaking the rules or not but why? Younger members of a community may be breaking the rules because, in fact, this is the only way that a community will move forward and do justice to its members. The rules may be broken because they are irrelevant or because they are no longer understood.

In all these circumstances real freedom demands that all those involved can do justice to their integrity as people. The superior has to preserve the ethos of the community, but to achieve this he or she has to share this responsibility with those appointed to help and also in consultation with the whole community. Consultation means, of course, much more than hearing another point of view. It demands comprehending it as far as is humanly possible. It would not be an exaggeration to state that whenever any one of us finds himself in a position of authority and cannot or will not comprehend the message that is being conveyed then we no longer respect the integrity of the other. So often this leads to the bitter cry — "He didn't understand". The complaint is no longer nowadays — "He did not listen". Equality and justice have ensured an extensive entitlement to be heard. But hearing is one thing, understanding is another and there can be no mutual integrity unless this is acknowledged. This is what is meant by meaningful communication.

It is, of course, impossible in such a rapidly changing world to comprehend fully the significance of alterations in priorities, values and nuances of life. But when we do not comprehend we have to recognise this. There is nothing more damaging to the integrity of human relationships than to use our freedom in communicating but only to show a new type of deafness. Having acquired in justice the right to be heard, much bitterness follows when it is felt that the words have fallen on deaf ears. The freedom to express ourselves requires also a response of integrity. This can be — "I don't understand" or "I do understand but cannot agree" or "I do understand and do agree but please be patient until we can overcome obstacle x,y,z," or "I don't understand and I may be wrong" or "I don't understand and I think you are wrong for all the following reasons" or "Let us agree to disagree". These are all exchanges of mutual integrity and contrast with — "I am sorry but you are wrong" or "I don't think you understand what you are saying or doing" — "I don't agree with your attitude and you will find no one else does" — "I don't understand what you are saying but in any case you are wrong" — "I don't like the way you are going about this. . . " or the worst response of all which is to feign agreement in order to avoid a confrontation.

Another small but important point emerges here. The freedom to communicate also requires in a Christian community not only a response of integrity but one of love. Loving in this situation means helping a person to discover as far as possible what it is they are truly concerned with. We have come to recognise, for example in industry, that workers may ask for money as the only visible expression of having other unfulfilled and unrecognised needs such as status, the avoidance of boredom, the opportunity for initiative, etc. So also in religious life people can use their newly acquired freedom of expression as a substitute for some other personal need much less clearly recognised. I shall refer in my second paper to our emotional needs for trust, receiving, giving, self-esteem and sexuality. It is possible that people are using some legitimate way of expressing themselves as a substitute for a different and deeper need and it is the task of their neighbour, and in particular of their superior, to help them to reach a more profound understanding of themselves. Integrity in community not only requires that we respond with justice to what is offered us but also that we help others to understand themselves more fully. Integrity of the moment anticipates an evolving self in which the meaning of the message is not fully comprehended for a period of months or even years. This is, after all, essential in our prayer in which God responds in the fullness of time. We, too, must be conscious of the depths of others so that we can respond to them with anticipatory wisdom, at the right time and in the right way. A combination of integrity and love also means that, even when we think we know the correct answer, we have to make sure that the other person is ready and capable of responding without being overwhelmed by anxiety at its implications. This was something clearly understood by our Lord who waited a long time for his public ministry and even then took great care not to paralyse people with the message he was offering. We have to avoid not only scandalising others but we have to show to them infinite patience both in helping them to understand themselves and also to avoid paralysing them with this discovery.

In this essay referring particularly to questions of freedom, I have stressed the need to recognise those physical, intellectual and social characteristics which need to be cherished and nurtured if we are fully to realise our potential. Such realisation inevitably needs the efficacious presence of others, and to do this we need to communicate effectively and with integrity. But even in the presence of the most effective communication − whether personal or social − we have to respect both the integrity of our feelings and those of others.

INTEGRITY AND PERSON II

In the previous essay an outline of integrity was given in terms of recognising our physical, intellectual and social potential and meeting it to the full. This is clearly one aspect of seeking the perfection of God's image in ourselves. Integrity, in this sense, has no finality for, as man's potential is constantly unfolding, it has a dynamic quality. In Christianity we believe that our Lord manifested in his human and divine nature the fullness of being which all members of his Body are seeking to attain and this they will do until the end of time.

> "Yes, you know me and you know where
> I come from.
> Yet I have not come of myself;
> No, there is one who sent me and I really come
> from Him and you do not know Him;
> but I know Him
> because I have come from Him
> and it was He who sent me."

John 7: 28-29

Just as in his previous statements our Lord could not deny his own integrity, there was no compromise regarding the reality of His Father and his special relationship with him described repeatedly in the gospels. As with our Lord, so with each one of us, our relationship to our parents is fundamental. There is a marked difference of course. Our Lord concentrated on his Father; we tend to emphasise our mother who remains the source of our first crucial experiences. It was so with our Lord, of course, but his origins and mission were unique. Nevertheless the gospels stress the overwhelming significance of personal attachment. All our Lord did, he did in obedience to a relationship of love between himself and his Father, indicating the closeness of the attachment.

Our humanity is also subject to these bonds of unique intimacy which we form with our mother and later with our father. At first these attachments are intensely physical. We have to recognise our mother with our eyes and ears and to receive a strong impression of our mutual reality through bodily contact. The body is thus at the centre, both of our own experience of ourselves and the means of forming attachments to others, and is a major force of communicating human integrity. It is also a challenge that needs to be faced in religious life which has hitherto considered the body with circumspection, if not outright alarm.

The Body and Relationship

In the first few years our principal experiences are mediated through the body. We are held by, and hold on to others, in events associated with feelings of safety, reassurance, comfort. The body is the principal medium through which anger and hostility are communicated and only gradually through socialisation are these feelings converted to verbal forms. Even then the body retains the muscular and nervous reactions associated with tension. We mete out and receive punishment with the body and use it as a powerful means of signalling forgiveness and reconciliation. The body is also the source of intense physical experiences in its various orifices and it is here that Sigmund Freud made his greatest contribution to an understanding of the human personality, doing so in instinctual terms which shocked and disgusted society. Christianity joined the chorus of protest and took special exception to the sexual implications of these themes.

Today, nearly three-quarters of a century after Freud's initial writings, we can examine these theories in perspective. The body is a vital source of gratification which we ignore or dismiss only at the risk of violating our integrity. The body is central to the communication of love, anger, sexuality and comfort. Christianity in general and religious life in particular has to come to terms with its significance.

I have been privileged to see and to talk to scores of religious and to consider in detail religious life in the last few years. From these experiences I have reached certain preliminary conclusions which I would like to consider with you.

First of all there is the question of the entry of new candidates to the religious life. It seems to me essential here that religious life does not become a haven for those who are afraid to experience their bodies. The term "experience their bodies" means that religious life should not accept women who are alienated from their body as a means of experiencing feelings of sex, anger or affection. It seems to me that screening processes which emphasise the social and intellectual aspects of candidates and ignore their physical and emotional maturity are doing a great disservice to the ideals of the religious life. These ideals should aim to attract whole people for whom religious life is neither an escape from nor a substitute for bodily and emotional integrity.

By bodily and emotional integrity I do not mean, incidentally, the absence of what are generally described as neurotic manifestations . I part company with those who are seeking statistical ideals with high intelligence, social aptness and complete freedom from physical and psychological complaints. If we excluded such men and women from other walks of life, society would be greatly impoverished.

The men and women who wish to serve Christ certainly need integrity, by which I understand awareness of themselves, and this should certainly include bodily awareness. They may be prone to fatigue, irritability, tension or moods. These are universal manifestations. It is really a question of degree. Those who seek religious life because they cannot cope with the ordinary demands of society have no place in it. But those who seek it, conscious of ordinary neurotic manifestations, which do not hamper them from discharging their obligations, are, in my opinion, suitable candidates to the religious life. It is the escape from the body and its neurotic manifestations by denying their existance that is a total contra-indication. The extended number of years before final vows have to be taken allows ample time to make continuous assessment of the candidate's maturity in this sphere.

By maturity in the bodily sphere I would also consider essential the ability to experience feelings of affection and sexuality and to be able to express them in a suitable manner. Clearly a suitable manner precludes an exclusive one-to-one relationship; this is precisely what marriage is, an exclusive one-to-one relationship between a man and a woman. This does not rule out in religious life intimate one-to-one relationships. It seems to me a violation of the integrity of human nature to consider that religious life has no place for affectionate bonds between individuals. In fact I would go so far as to say that the man or woman who is incapable of having intimate one-to-one relationships has no place in the religious life. The ability to form such bonds is a continuation of the one-to-one relationships we had with our parents, and is also a mark of human integrity.

In these one-to-one relationships body and mind need to harmonise with our feelings, and find expression in an acceptable social manner. Such one-to-one relationships will prove a source of personal reassurance, of self-confidence, and self-awareness. From these one-to-one relationships there emerges the strength to care for and to love others. We cannot love others unless we have been first loved ourselves, which usually occurs in childhood but needs constant renewal in our one-to-one relationships.

Two principal fears have haunted us in the past. First, that exclusive relationships will lead to homosexuality. It seems to me that, if a person is a homosexual and needs to express this in overt sexual physical terms, then he or she has no place in the religious life. But this fear has damaged the opportunities of the overwhelming majority of people who are perfectly capable of intimate affection without endangering their sexual integrity. Religious, like everyone else, should have the freedom to experience their sexuality in appropriate human form. They have selected not to exercise its physical expression in marriage or in homosexual relationships. This is the vow of chastity. But chastity does not mean denial of sexuality and, indeed, if religious are going to reach others in an abundance of devoted understanding, they cannot isolate themselves from this vital dimension of human integrity. The second fear has been that "special friendships" – as they used to be called – will fragment the community atmosphere. There is evidence from innumerable sources that community life can be an artefact in which apparently everybody mixes but no one is really able to get close to each other because personal bonds do not exist. This alienation in the midst of a supposed closely knit atmosphere is being strongly criticised by religious who feel the lack of integrity resulting in these circumstances. Community life is like a family. There have to be personal bonds in which some members are united by the affinity of kindred interests or personal attraction. These relationships will grow and form the rock-like foundations to which the individuals concerned will return repeatedly for personal growth, renewal and sustenance. If they are effective they will provide the additional dynamism to reach and love others with whom there are fewer links of mutual attraction.

Expression of Feelings

It is in the presence of these intimate relationships that certain aspects of the pesonality will emerge. We all know how difficult it is for some to show their feelings in group situations. They can only do so in the safe seclusions of a trusted one-to-one relationship.

It is only in such close relationships that our fears of inadequacy and inferiority can be freely revealed. None of us can escape these anxieties, and human integrity needs to recognise and deal with their presence. All of us are assailed by doubts of our efficiency, competence, intelligence, social aptness and suitability for certain tasks. There is a need to share such anxieties without fear of being ridiculed or humiliated, which means being listened to with care and, as I said in the previous essay, we need a response that can allay our fears and help us to regain confidence. A good deal of human love is expressed in helping others to recognise their gifts and encourage them to develop these fully. You may note that this is at variance with the usual message so familiar, namely to become conscious of our faults and to change. We certainly need to do that, but often we are far more conscious of our faults, limitations and defects than our creative, positive, fruitful selves. We need others to discover these qualities and repeatedly confirm them in us. As our confidence grows so does our security and our self-esteem, and we spend less energy being preoccupied with protecting ourselves from the real or imaginary accusations and criticism of others. The more positive our own image becomes, the greater is our freedom to love others. The less preoccupied we are with our own survival, the greater is our availability to others.

In the past we reached the same conclusion by emphasising the avoidance of introspection, self-centredness, attention to oneself. This, in my view, was only a half truth and missed a vital aspect of human integrity. Caring for others when we live a personal life of deprivation, uncertainty, fear, insecurity and dissatisfaction leads ultimately to disaster. We come to resent, envy, even hate the well-being of others which we provide but do not possess ourselves. We need to receive, to increase in our wholeness in order to be really effective in meeting the needs of others.

In order to achieve this, what is required is the ability to express, receive and incorporate feelings of worthiness, approval and commendation. Far too many people are aware of criticism, disapproval, rejection and do not know how to recognise, appreciate nor accept messages of praise. Similarly some find it very difficult to show feelings of joy and pleasure towards others. To give and to receive such feelings is an essential aspect of human integrity.

Initiative

Giving anything to others requires both freedom and initiative. In the previous essay reference was made to our increasing awareness of the social aspects of freedom. All the new constitutions of religious life are careful to stress the dignity, freedom and wide area of personal responsibility. These measures are simply ensuring that the significance given to man by a humanitarian world is not lacking in our religious communities. It is said that in these matters of human integrity the Church has had to be led and guided by others and this is part of the pain we have had to endure in the last decade when we discovered just how alienated the Catholic Church had become from the legitimate advances of human nature. It had been a severe test of faith which has tried many sorely. But now we must look to the future and again take the lead in showing human beings the truth of our integrity. A great deal of this will be found in the discoveries of psychology which go beyond social change.

Human beings have claimed — and rightly — increasing freedom in the expression of their rights. The basic rights to work, security, equality, education, freedom of speech and leisure are slowly becoming the fabric of Western societies and as a result of this clarification any violation of human dignity can be discerned more accurately. Perhaps one of the most hopeful signs of 1970 was the way in which world opinion helped commute sentences in both Spain and Russia. But in the smaller spheres of home, office and community life, freedom has to be exercised by individuals who have their own limited personal capacities.

One of these limitations of which dynamic psychology is very conscious is the individual's inability to feel free and to take initiative in the presence of ample social freedom. This is a phenomenon which we know from other activities. There is universal suffrage, but at the very best only 70-80 per cent of people vote, and voting on many other lesser occasions is even more limited. Having acquired freedom we need to be free psychologically and suitably motivated to exercise our freedom. In theory every member of a religious community should be contributing his or her personal share to its life. In order to achieve this a person needs to feel that he has something good and positive to contribute and feels confident enough to take the initiative to do so.

Taking the initiative demands a certain psychological balance, for instance, a person has to feel he is an individual in his own right. Authoritarian structures do not come about simply because strong men and women set out deliberately to control others. There is often a collusion between those who find leadership, initiative, decision-making painful and those who find it fulfilling and seek it. It is true that human beings can be roughly divided into extroverts and introverts, but there are innumerable gradations which qualify this statement. The introvert, shy, quiet person may be bubbling with intense feelings and ideas inside, and the extrovert, who on the surface appears full of confidence and certainty, may be markedly anxious underneath. The point I am making is that authoritarian structures are established by the abandonment, the abdication of initiative on the part of the many in favour of the few. This can also be a continuation of childhood dependence on authority.

Whether it is emotional dependence emanating from a continuation of childhood or an aspect of introversion, human integrity demands that the person should reach a basic minimum of personal initiative and independence which will allow them to communicate to others their inner world. External freedom needs to be matched by an equivalent internal one and human integrity requires this balance. Whether people wish to exercise their freedom is a complex matter ultimately to be decided by themselves alone, but they should aim to attain the freedom to be in a position to do so. This aspect of the personality has a special significance in religious life.

Community life should be so arranged that the emotional dependence of its members should gradually give way to a growing independence so that as far as possible every member of the community is capable of feeling and relating to others as adults. This means organising community life on a basis in which personal responsibility for one's self and for the community as a whole is kept at the forefront of religious life. Ultimately religious should not feel that they compare in any way unfavourably with the whole range of personal responsibilities and

41

rewards of those pursuing other vocations. But, like life in the family, this degree of independence and initiative needs constant nurturing and renewal. Such nurturing and renewal will emanate from a balance between growth achieved in personal relationships and opportunities for common interchange. Community life should aim deliberately at constructing appropriate goals for the growth and development of initiative. In practice this means fewer decisions from authority not based on discussion, more experimentation, more encouragement of personal decision, even at, the risk of mistakes being made. There is a far greater danger of over-protection, a disease from which the Church is just beginning to convalesce. Over-protection and infantilisation have played havoc with human integrity.

There are those, however, whose restraint is not childish fear. Their personality is so constructed that uttering a sentence publicly reduces them to a state of panic. Such a personal handicap should be quickly recognised and appreciated by others. Anxiety is a common phenomenon and frequently a sign of neurosis. There are many men and women handicapped by features of anxiety as shown by their blushing, stammering, blinking, inability to complete a sentence or even to start one. These features are certainly no evidence of unsuitability for religious life. When they are alone or in smaller groups or in one-to-one relationships such people may show a serenity and certainty totally obscured by the public occasion. It is this internal maturity that religious life should be seeking to attract to its ranks, even though it is covered by layers of anxiety manifestations. Anxiety in any case can be reduced by encouraging such people to participate by degrees in the sort of activity which is initially anxiety provoking. The reassuring support of others will act as a stimulus to reduce the anxiety which will be slowly eliminated. Those familiar with teaching will know all the techniques used to foster confidence and initiative in the classroom. These approaches, suitably modified, should be used constantly.

Anger

The capacity to feel emotionally independent also requires an understanding of the place of anger in human relationships.

In the authoritarian relationship anger is legitimate in one direction only, from above downwards. The reverse was considered disrespectful, cheeky, an indication of a complete failure to understand the meaning of obedience. These judgements were aided and abetted by the child-parent relationship which existed between the person in authority and the community. Anger in this relationship meant attacking the source of security and love and carried with it overtones of damaging the source which sustained life. It carried a quality of guilt which punished far more severely internally than any external punishment. Finally to

42

fear and guilt is added in some people a sense of permanency and irreversibility. Children who grew up in homes where punishment was inflicted by withdrawal of the parent learned the hell of feeling cut off from the vital source of their existence and lived with the permanent threat of such a catastrophe deep inside them.

All these and other reasons make people suppress and repress their anger. Suppression is a voluntary, conscious action, repression is an unconscious process. At this point I am often confronted by the incredulous gasp of people who cannot really believe that anything good can be achieved by altering these patterns of inhibition.

Just before the Jewish Passover, Jesus went up to Jerusalem and in the Temple he found people selling cattle and sheep and pigeons and the money changers sitting at their counters there. Making a whip out of some cord, He drove them all out of the Temple, cattle and sheep as well, scattered the money changers' coins, knocked their tables over and said to pigeon sellers — "Take all this out of here and stop turning my Father's house into a market."'

John 2: 13-16

Christ had no inhibitions in expressing his anger. In doing so he was showing with his body, his action, and through words his intense dis-approval of the way the Temple was being prostituted. Anger is a means of declaring that our integrity is being violated. Much has to be learned about anger. We have to discern which violations of our personality are central and which peripheral. We could get angry at regular intervals throughout the day. In these circumstances we would fail in the pur-pose of anger, which is a sharp alerting signal to others to take notice of our existence. If we lost our temper over every triviality we would also lose the value of scarcity. Similarly, showing anger as a means of reliev-ing feelings of pent-up tension has its uses, but it can be an unconstruc-tive self-indulgence. Anger needs to be constructive and ideally it should be addressed to those that matter in our lives so that they can take cognizance of our grievance and, if justified, alter their behaviour towards us. I am no advocate of the indiscriminate release of anger for its own sake, although those who are learning to be angry in adult life for the first time may be initially non-discriminating. Not all anger will prove self-justifying. We shall discover that our anger has been aroused as a result of misunderstandings, misconstructions, undue sensitivity on our part, faulty and imperfect communication. To anger must be added the capacity to feel and express guilt, sorrow, remorse. For some these are acutely painful feelings crowded with memories of humiliation in the past. The pain may be so acute that both anger and reconciliation are avoided. Such a situation is understandable but denies the essentials of human integrity which must recognise anger, guilt and reconciliation as part and parcel of being human. In this respect we can love others in a special way when they have offended us unjustifiably. We can help them to draw near to us afresh without expressing indignity and humility. This is not a question of being generous at times of victory nor a matter of condescending bounty. Much more than this, it involves our ability to feel the intense pain, guilt, confusion, anxiety of others and, in accepting it, offer at the same time the means of reducing its intensity. Yes, they have offended us but their personal significance is not marred, their image remains untarnished. Such an approach requires the ability to tolerate at close proximity the pain and distress of others so that, in recognising and sharing it with them, we give them a realistic awareness that they are not so bad, wicked, nasty as they feel. Yes, they are in the wrong, but this is a matter of individual actions, it is not a rejection of their whole self which they feel. Forgiveness and reparation which is at the very heart of the Christian message implies all this and it has to be lived from moment to moment in religious life as indeed in all Christian life which aims at the constant imitation of Christ.

Summary

I want to conclude with a brief summary of what I have been trying to convey in these two essays. We all start life as a tiny but separate existence. Our development is a continuous expression of gradual separation from our parents. This separation reaches its conclusion in the second half of the second decade of life. Through its laws and customs society attempts to safeguard the principles of this independence. People can now marry at eighteen without parental permission, they can also vote at this age and a myriad other prescribed conditions continuously assess and safeguard the dignity and significance of the individual. All this comes under the science of sociology. But, within this social framework of reference, human beings have to feel and express themselves psychologically. They have to discover their own separate existence physically, intellectually and, above all, emotionally. They need to retain their own integrity as unique individuals in giving and receiving of themselves. The principle that must govern such exchanges is enshrined for Christianity in the law of love. Loving God, our neighbours and ourselves sums up our faith but needs to be translated in the concrete awareness of ourselves and of ourselves in relation to others.

Loving means being aware of our bodies, intellects and feelings and seeking the realisation of their potential in a way that we do not infringe our own or the legitimate rights of others. We do not have a perfect formula for this, but we are learning all the time what human integrity implies. It means safeguarding our individuality so that when we offer care, support, encouragement, affection, love or anger to others we do not lose our separate selves and become part of them. This requires a balance between closeness and separation so that we can get close to others with our bodies, minds and feelings but do not become trapped by their demands so that we lose ourselves. The Christian teaching of losing ourselves in order to find ourselves means such total and safe possession of ourselves that no matter what treatment we receive from others, however hostile, rejecting, degrading or suffocating, however much we may lose our external image, nonetheless we retain our inner core of sameness and certainty. The more we possess this the more we can get lost in the needs of others and yet discover and give more of ourselves. Our Lord portrays the truth of this with singular clarity.

"I am the bread of life;
He who comes to me will never be hungry;
He who believes in me will never thirst;
But, as I have told you,
You can see me and still you do not believe.
All that the Father gives me will come to me,
and whoever comes to me
I shall not turn him away;
because I have come from heaven,
not to do my own will
but to do the will of the one who sent me.
Now the will of Him who sent me
is that I shall lose nothing
of all that He has given to me;
and that I should raise it up on the last day.
Yes, it is my Father's will
that whoever sees the Son and believes in Him
shall have eternal life,
and that I shall raise him on the last day."

John 6: 34-40

Such total affirmation of himself allows Christ to declare his total integrity. He expresses total obedience to the will of the Father and in this he discovers all that He is. It is through this total and separate existence that he possesses his whole self and gives it to all others. In an analogous manner we give ourselves to others totally preserving and deepening our own integrity in the process. And as St John tells us, our Lord will lose nothing and shall raise all of us in the last day.

Through faith we, too, live in this life. Faith is really nothing less than our trust in the integrity of Christ. But through the Incarnation this integrity lives in all of us here and now and human integrity has as much relevance in our day as on the last day of time.

PART II

In part II there are six essays. The first draws attention to the importance, when speaking of the spiritual life, of using language which describes and incorporates the whole person, with particular emphasis on the body. The subsequent essays then take up the themes of marriage and the single state and develop their significance in the light of our changing awareness of "fulness" in the inner life. The essays on *Marriage and the Single State* were given to a conference of superiors at Spode House, *Single State, Community and Perfection* to a Congregation of Sisters and *Emotional Maturity and the Priesthood* was commissioned by, and first appeared in, the Clergy Review.

BODY AND SOUL

The title of this paper is one that has challenged Western thought throughout most of its recorded history. Since I am neither a historian nor a philosopher, my primary task is not to consider in detail the theological and philosophical developments of these two key words. My paper will be devoted to the living experience of Roman Catholics, indeed of most Christians, who have grown up with an all-pervading notion that the essence of Christianity is to "Save one's soul." This phrase echoes and re-echoes in the heart of Christendom and the opposition between soul and body is an equally familiar refrain which will be considered in this paper. It is worth recalling briefly some of the principal features of what we call our soul.

The language of what follows is philosophical in character and points to one of the central features of recent life in the Church; namely the ascendancy of abstract, metaphysical terminology which described man in undoubtedly authentic but virtually incomprehensible terms for the overwhelming majority of the people of God. I wish to illustrate this from as recent a work as *Sacramentum Mundi,* an encyclopaedia of theology.

'The soul itself is not man. . . It is one of his principles of being. . . It is substantial in character, contrary to the assertion of psychological actualism. As partial cause (formal, because a principle) of (the whole of) human nature, it stands in a primordial relationship to its material, corporeal constitution. The material principle, to which the soul essentially belongs, as its form, can be designated as the 'prime substance' of the soul, on account of its priority to it, even genetically. When it reflects materiality itself (and not just some material object), it gains distance, as in the anima soul, and then when the specific difference intervenes, when the reflection is substantial, it is called spirit. It is independent in character, though its essence is always intrinsically determined by its origin, which is also the reason of its individuality. . . As spirit, it is the intrinsic form of the body and so possesses a so-called natural immortality.' (*Sacramentum Mundi* Vol. vi p.138).

I find this paragraph virtually incomprehensible and would venture to suggest that this would be the verdict of anyone without a philosophical training. So what, may come the reply. Would not a psychological or psychoanalytical statement be equally confusing to the non-expert? In defence I could reply that this would depend on the writer and the care taken to consider the expertise of the audience. Psychological statements can certainly be made perfectly intelligible to a non-expert audience. But with the word soul, we are here dealing with a central theological concept, widely utilised as a symbol and reality, which evokes spiritual motivation in the heart of the Christian. Clearly the gap between its everyday use, with which we are familiar, and the above, philosophical description, is immense, indeed the gap can hardly be bridged.

One of the facts contributing to the present plight of Christianity is precisely this distance between the everyday experience of Christians and the offical symbolic language of the Church which is meant to lead us to God.

When the aura of all things sacred was attacked by an age that had become deeply suspicious of authority and its apparently empty slogans, Christians, thrown sharply on the defensive, could not cope and retreated hastily. The scientific humanist said that he could neither observe nor justify the idea of the human soul and therefore could not believe in it. Such expectations are absurd, replied the theologian; but the definition of the soul in philosophical terms became absurd in a different way. It stood its ground rationally but it became irrelevant for all but the few.

Its relevance, on the other hand, assumed familiar characteristics and lived on in the common mind much as before. Let us examine two popular meanings of the word.

The soul somehow became the opposite of the body; this meant that Christians had to contend with dichotomy in their everyday lives. Religion was expressed as something separate which involved going to church on Sunday, avoiding sin and saying prayers. Most of this behaviour was emotionally associated with the soul, the spiritual principle of man, detached and separated from the secular routine, from the mundane experiences of life. This rigid division of life into activities of the 'body' and 'soul' became deeply enmeshed in the life of all Christians who thus ran the risk of falling into a schizophrenic existence. Nor was this exercise confined to church-going activities but extended into the cultural sphere being found in both literature and music. Take, for example, Elgar's *Dream of Gerontius* which is a vivid and magnificent musical interpretation of the soul's last journey.

The advantages of such a readily available, vivid and intensely descriptive "phraseology" are obvious and the word soul came to be used as the most convenient term to describe the God-orientated activity of man. But words can become dangerously empty and this is precisely what has happened to our spiritual vocabulary; we can no longer simply turn to the past to tap rich sources of communication. When we use the word 'soul' to-day, it hardly evokes spontaneous chords of awe or brings to mind man's closest links with God.

The soul was not only intimately related to man's religious activities, as opposition to the non-religious, but carried a further specific element of significance. If soul and body were recognized as separate and opposite elements, then clearly the body was inferior, of lesser importance, played a secondary role and was required, through sacrifice and deprivation, to serve the interests of the soul. This diminishing of the body's significance in favour of the soul is something of which every Christian is all too well aware. The dangers of the body have often been described. What Christian does not recognise the risks involved in ignoring the Church's warnings against sexual indulgence, greed, and personal wealth? The body, if not treated as specifically evil, came at least to be regarded with suspicion. However, this suspicion was at times extreme, particularly in the area of sexuality. Once again the current response has been first to question the validity of such an attitude and then simply to ignore it. Inevitably the reaction has been intense in some quarters where excess is seen as a solution to the puritanism of the past. While Christianity must not accept a new distortion of human integrity it must, at the same time, correct its own serious disregard for the significance of the body.

The body-soul dichotomy and the deliberate diminution of bodily significance with the emphasis on its dangers have been widely held convictions which have nurtured our Christian upbringing for generations. For a while the Church attacked the counter movements in society as dangerous instruments of modernism but, in the end, a whole new perspective has prevailed which is clearly summed up in Article 14 of *Gaudium et Spes* of Vatican II.

'Though made of body and soul, man is one. Through his bodily composition he gathers to himself the elements of the material world. Thus they reach their crown through him, and through him raise their voice in free praise of the Creator.

For this reason man is not allowed to despise his bodily life. Rather, he is obliged to regard his body as good and honourable since God has created it and will raise it up on the last day. Nevertheless, wounded by sin, man experiences rebellious stirrings in his body. But the very dignity of man postulates that man glorify God in his body and forbid it to serve the evil inclinations of his heart.

Now, man is not wrong when he regards himself as superior to bodily concerns, and as more than a speck of nature or a nameless constituent of the city of man. For by his interior qualities he outstrips the whole sum of mere things. He finds re-enforcement in this profound insight whenever he enters into his own heart. God, who probes the heart, awaits him there. . . . . When man recognises in himself a spiritual and immortal soul, he is not being mocked by a deceptive fantasy springing from mere physical or social influences. On the contrary he is getting to the depths of the very truth of the matter.

Article 14 of *Gaudium et Spes*.

It is of note that, in the collected documents of Vatican II covering some seven hundred pages, the word "soul" occurs rarely, and in the index only once, from the passage just quoted. But, if the word is no longer used as a short-circuit process to describe Christian life, it has still a crucial place and there have been dogmatic definitions about it.

Thus we are taught that man has a soul which exists as a separate and unique entity and is immortal. Each soul is created by God directly from nothing but is not part of the divine substance and has neither pre-corporeal existence nor a material origin. It is the vital principle in man, is higher than the body, is destined after death and before the resurrection to experience the essence of God and ultimately its immortality ensures the completion of the whole person in a mysterious way which involves the body.

While all these declarations on the soul are as relevant to-day as when they were first formulated, the Council has shifted the emphasis away from the dichotomy of body and soul, and the inherent ambiguity of these words, towards a more comprehensive terminology, man frequently being described by the word person.

'The Council brings to mankind light kindled from the gospel, and puts at its disposal those saving resources which the Church herself, under the guidance of the Holy Spirit, receives from her Founder. For the human person deserves to be preserved; human society deserves to be renewed. Hence the pivotal point of our total presentation will be man himself, whole and entire, body and soul, heart and conscience, mind and will.'

Article 3 of *Gaudium et Spes*.

This passage highlights two features which will revolutionise the life of the Church. First, the emphasis is no longer on abstract, metaphysical considerations but on the light kindled from the gospel. It is the incarnate Word, the second person of the Trinity, the mystery of one person and two natures that becomes the living source of everyday immediate Christian consideration. Secondly, attention is focused on human beings as whole persons living a full life here and now. The schism of body and soul which has hitherto afflicted Christian life at all levels, personal and social, has been resolved. The next world once had a fascinating and distinctive significance, as opposed to the present one, and we were comforted by the thought that this vale of tears would pass and give way to an idyllic heaven in which suffering and conflict were unknown. Such a philosophy of life had dangerous implications for the plight of man in his earthly state and undoubtedly gave impetus to the materialistic philosophy of Marxism which saw religion as the opium of the people.

Now both Vatican II and our society as a whole stress that the human person deserves to be preserved and renewed. Our life is no longer simply a painful sentence which seeks release in death.

This new vision is precisely what humanist thinking has been advocating for a long period and the former opposition of Christianity to it was clearly sadly mistaken. But, of course, the teaching on man and his integrated nature extends beyond simple humanism for, living through faith, we become conscious of Christ who leads the way to the Father and who promised to send the Spirit which would remain in the midst of God's people witnessing truth.

The implications of these changes are enormous and will take time to percolate through our lives. Indeed the recognition of the importance of the features of man in no way diminishes the difficulties of attaining to that state. But now the goal is far clearer, especially so far as the body is concerned. Christianity must now attend to the body's welfare with as much concern and involvement as it has always shown when dealing with the mind.

What are some of the practical implications if this goal is to be pursued rigorously?

It means that the priority now given, in all societies, to people's material welfare must become a Christian priority. Wherever the Church finds itself in a situation where social injustices are being perpetrated, it has to declare its unconditional opposition to them. No longer should anyone be in a position to point a finger of accusation at the Church as an upholder of those forces which materially exploit the poor for the profit of powerful minorities.

Acceptance of the uninterrupted progress of material standards is in itself a process which has moral complexities. It is easy to identify those parts of the world whose poverty is still rife but what about a country like ours which has a high standard of living? How is this to be preserved? Who pays the cost? Who is to protect those who cannot exert strong economic influence to gain financial advantages? Are we to find, in the presence of material affluence, a relentless and selfish quest for more without due regard to the economic capacities of the country as a whole? Are the strong unions to be allowed to pursue their interests at the expense of the less powerful ones? These and other questions are the moral issues of the future. They bring the Christian into a direct involvement with the economic and political life of the country, as a direct consequence of treating man as a whole person rooted in the historicity of our times. There can be no opting out into a Sunday church attendance routine which absolves our responsibilities for the rest of the week.

This is a new political involvement for the Christian now no longer concerned with power politics to safeguard the status and power of the Church as a social organ of effective control.

"This sacred Synod proclaims the highest destiny of man and champions the godlike seed which has been sown in him. It offers to mankind the honest assistance of the Church in fostering that brotherhood of all men... Inspired by no earthly ambition, the Church seeks but a solitary goal: to carry forward the work of Christ Himself under the lead of the befriending Spirit. And Christ entered this world to give witness to the truth, to reassure and not to sit in judgement, to serve and not to be served."

Article 3 of *Gaudium et Spes.*

Christ entered the world to give witness to the truth, a truth which the whole person lives through their everyday experience. This truth is not dependent on his state of nutrition or malnutrition, housing condition, educational facilities, secure employment, material security.

It exists independently of material progress but men encounter God in and through these experiences and, the more consistent and fitting they are with his dignity, the richer becomes the opportunity to see the image of God unfold. Thus the Christian betrays nothing of his faith in engaging in improving living standards, provided that this does not exclude the vision of God who is the source of all fulfillment. But the vision of God is never threatened by material progress interpreted correctly as an unfolding of man's possibility to attain the richness of God's vision for him.

The duality between the religious and the secular now ceases, for the whole person expresses the Christian message, wherever they are, twenty four hours a day. The sacramental and liturgical encounter with Christ is a process of essential renewal for the life of faith but its meaning must extend throughout the week. Human encounter with the living Christ at mass is an event affecting the whole life in which body, mind and heart experience God at a precise moment which is a continuation of the past and a preparation for the future. The encounter with God is not periodic, it is continuous in the same way that a person's life is continuous.

If this is to be achieved, then the body which is central to our living experience of ourselves must have an appropriate significance of its own. Politics is the means for bringing about major changes which influence the material standards of living. But, beyond these social changes, there is a moment to moment experience of the body which is determined by our attitude to it. Given that minimum standards exist which allay hunger and thirst, prevent disease and provide shelter, we are all left with a body which is no longer threatened with extinction. After physical survival, there is an infinite possibility of bodily satisfaction, gratification and fulfillment which has inspired massive fears in Christian thought in the past. The danger of bodily gratification overwhelming man's spirit is a recurrent theme met by a mixture of active denial and sacrificial process.

The risk of self-indulgence in food, drink and sex have reverberated from pulpits and Christian writing for centuries in the sincere belief that, if the body is held in check, the soul will flourish. This view could not be further from the truth. The encounter with God is that of a whole person in which the body plays a central role. Its denial in no way ensures a better relationship with God and, indeed in the area of sexuality, it has in fact actively impoverished Christian life most severely.

The Gospels showed most clearly that our Lord did not ignore the significance of food, hence his miracles of the multiplication of the loaves and the fish, nor the place of entertainment, hence his presence as a guest at numerous celebrations; nor the significance of drink as witnessed by his desire to have his own thirst assuaged by the woman near the well and the first miracle of the changing of water to wine at the wedding of Cana. His attitude to sex showed all the characteristics of compassion, acceptance and the fullest possible demonstration of human integrity. He knew, both as God and as man, the importance of human sexuality as a means of expressing love. He did not underestimate its strength, which can convert love into exploitation, but, whenever he was confronted by people in sexual disarray, he took good care to safeguard sexuality by reminding them that they had to avoid sin; that is to say to use their sexuality in a fully human way.

In this respect Christianity can do no better than to return to its most loving source, Christ himself, and there rediscover the meaning of sexuality. There, the body with its capacity to see, hear, touch, receive, give, fuse, separate, procreate, nurture and to experience delights of pleasure and contentment, has a central place which Christianity has a sacred duty not only to proclaim loudly and clearly but to champion as forcefully as possible. Only by such unequivocal declaration of its faith in the body as the most precious instrument of communicating love, can it go on to show the world that chastity, preserving sexual integrity, is a natural and desirable concomitant.

But preoccupation with the instincts of self-preservation does not exhaust the possibility of the body. Modern medicine and psychology have shown us the depth of richness in the structure of the body and its ability to provide us with the means responsible for cognition and conation. The utter dependence of the human person on the perfect functioning of the body, particularly the brain, can be seen most clearly in the unconscious patient who, while still alive in the fullest sense, is completely unable to express his humanity. This does not mean that the body can fully exhaust the meaning of man but beyond it we are in the realm of faith, a faith which we must not forget demanded the Incarnation. If ever we needed a reminder of the link between faith and body, the life of the second person of the Trinity furnishes the answer.

Christ's life was centred on a relationship between himself, the Father and the Spirit. His relationship with the Father was crucial and the continuous dialogue between himself and the Father in a relationship of love is the model for our relationship between ourselves and God. As Christ related himself fully -- body and soul -- to the Father and the Spirit, so we too, in Christ, have to live the same relationship with the Trinity. Christ's body experienced the whole range of physical possibilities apart from marital sexuality and our body likewise has to seek the same level of intensity.

In Christ we know that the fullness of human life is to be found. The gospels show unequivocally that Christ never undervalued the body with which he communicated his message of love and redemption. Such complete acceptance of the body in the Incarnate Word is a guarantee that our relationship with God beyond death will not suffer if the body receives its full recognition here and now.

Indeed it is through the full acceptance of the meaning of the Incarnation in which the human nature of the second person received the full imprint of its potentiality that we can recognize and share the richness of the body. In doing so we can acknowledge with gratitude the attention drawn to the body by our humanist friends and, at the same time, invite them to see a dimension of meaning which the cross and the resurrection supply and without which man's full significance cannot be recognised.

Christ chose to love us fully in the Incarnation. In return He asks us to cherish a new commandment which is to love one another as He loved us. In order to respond to this invitation fully we must pay as much regard to our bodies as did God who, from the depths of eternity, knew that the fullness of His love required an incarnate expression.

THE FUTURE OF CHRISTIAN MARRIAGE

When Christians of all denominations look at the contemporary scene of marriage they find much which is disturbing: there are several problems which appear at first sight to have no decisive, clear solutions. I would like to begin by cataloguing these challenges, examine some of their causes and finally formulate a concept of marriage which, in my opinion, can form the basis of future developments.

Attacks Against Marriage:

There are frontal and subtle attacks against marriage and each one has to be taken seriously.

a) The death of marriage:

The most radical but least popular view is the abolition of marriage. Marriage as a life-long, monogamous union has been attacked from three principal sources.

Part of Marxist philosophy but not of practice has been to condemn marriage as a class exploitation phenomenon. Friedrich Engels stated most clearly the theoretical objection to marriage in terms of class oppression:

"The first class antagonism appearing in history coincides with the development of the antagonism of man and wife in monogamy, and the first class oppression with that of the female by the male sex. Monogamy was a great historical progress. But by the side of slavery and private property it marks at the same time the epoch, which reaching down to our days, takes with all progress, also a step backwards, relatively speaking, and develops the welfare and advancement of one by the woe and submission of the other."

F. Engels, *Private Property and the State.*

This uncompromising view has also been taken up understandably by some of the more extreme elements of the women's liberation movement.

And finally a small group of psychiatrists in this country have written extensively about the damage that marriage does to the members of the family. The most outspoken of these critics is Dr. D. Cooper in his book the *Death of the Family,* but in more subtle ways Dr. R.

56

Laing (*The Politics of the Family*) has described mechanisms of making one individual in the family a scapegoat for the rest or of driving a person to the point of madness. In fairness it should be added that most psychiatrists would not accept that these observations point to more than a fraction of the root causes of that severe form of mental illness known as schizophrenia, but the point has been raised and certainly should be acknowledged.

b) The relaxation of sexual discipline:

There is another group of modifications offered by others who do not wish to destroy marriage itself but to relax all the restrictions of pre-marital and extra-marital sexual conduct so that fornication, adultery, spouse swapping, threesomes, quartet arrangements and, if necessary, the backing of abortion, all become part of normal living.

c) Easier divorce:

Still staying within the acceptance of marriage as a desired norm there are those who believe that divorce should be made reasonably easy and the concept of monogamy considered as a useful but hardly essential principle to be strictly observed. Looking at the statistics the incidence of marital breakdown is apparently increasing by leaps and bounds. The word 'apparently' has been used because scientific caution is required here. Certainly the figures, measured by petitions presented to the court, have risen at an alarming rate recently.

New petitions filed	
1901-1905	4,062
1931-1935	23,921
1947	48,501
1958	26,239
1969	61,216
1971	110,017

These figures show that after an expected post-war rise there was a fall until the late fifties since when there has been a decisive rise which cannot be explained away by any coincidental rise for instance, in the size of population. The rise in 1971 may be partially accounted for by the operation of the first full year of the new Divorce Act but there is evidence to suggest that the increase existed before and is likely to remain a permanent feature of the foreseeable future. In fact the total size of breakdown has been calculated to be as high as one-sixth to one-quarter of all marriages in England and Wales. The real problem, and one that does not admit to easy solutions, is whether marital breakdown in terms of separation — formal and informal — desertion or simply the presence of two people living together under the same roof without a conjugal relationship, the so-called empty shell marriage, has always been at this high level or whether only in recent years people have decided to take legal action and seek alternative solutions.

Whatever the answer may be, it is one that should cause concern to all, but particularly Christians committed as part of their faith to the ideal of stable life-long unions. Disquiet is one thing, understanding and prevention is another. Much of the reaction of the Christian community has been to try to return to traditional standards and mobilise a greater respect for familiar moral principles. The attack on all forms of permissiveness is precisely this combination of censure and appeal for a return to moral law. And yet it has to be admitted that the response is a limited one. People are certainly looking for the truth, there is no doubt about that. But the familiar sounds evoke little response and the admonitions fall on deaf ears.

What is needed is not innovation for the sake of innovation but a grasp of reality at a deeper level. In the case of marriage we have to recognise that in many respects there have been tremendous changes which need recognising and adjusting to. Let us look at some of these.

Changing Characteristics of Marriage:

a) Duration of marriage

The duration of marriage depends on the age at which two people marry and how long they are expected to live. On both these scores our century has seen changes, of which human longevity is clearly the more dramatic of the two. Looking at the Registrar General's statistics we can see that nearly twenty-five years have been added to the average expectation of life since the turn of the century when the average expectation of life in 1900 was 44.1 for a man 47.8 for a woman and today the respective figures are 68.5 and 74.8. When this is coupled with a younger age of marriage we discover the first startling fact, namely that contemporary marriages can be expected to last much longer than those of previous generations. It has been calculated that the average duration of marriage in 1911 was 28 years as compared to 42 years in 1967. In fact, from now on fifty years of marriage will certainly be an average expectation and not the exception.

b) Children

The expansion of the duration of marriage coincides with another important change. In the past the parents could be expected to die when they had seen their children — or at least some of them — through adolescence and thus their main function of carrying on the human race was fulfilled. Not only was this responsibility executed but in many ways childbearing and child rearing occupied the central part of their marriage, both in terms of time, energy and the years the parents could be expected to live. It is not surprising that Christianity saw children as a primary end of matrimony to which all the devotion of the parents should be directed.

But childbearing and rearing has also seen a transformation in our day. Medicine has made such important strides in the care of mother and child that many fewer pregnancies are required to ensure the desirable number of living children, thus freeing much time for both parents but particularly for the mother. The figures for infant mortality, i.e. deaths under the age of one year, which were 129.4 per 1,000 live births in 1911, became 18 in 1969, together with those relating to still births, 41 per 1000 live births in 1931, 13 in 1969, are unarguable data in this matter.

Not only has childbearing become safer and earlier but the number of children required to populate the world is less. The world is no longer threatened with under-population and this, coupled with the widespread advent of birth control, means that childbearing — the single most important event which engaged the life of married partners in the past — will no longer do so in the future. Children will of course remain vitally important but, as the size of the family is reduced, the emphasis will undoubtedly shift to the relationship of the spouses and the quality of their life styles. In other words, we have to address ourselves to the question of what will marriage do for the partners themselves apart from giving them the unique privilege of being parents on which so much of the essence of marriage depended until recently.

c) The Husband-Wife bond

Here in many ways we come to the heart of the matter. For centuries, indeed for thousands of years, in Western society the husband-wife bond has depended on fairly clearly delineated roles which have been handed down by tradition and they are worth spelling out. The husband was recognised as the head of the family, its leader to whom obedience and respect were owed by the wife and the children. He had the responsibility of looking after the family, protecting it from external threats, ensuring its material survival and taking the appropriate decisions in order to ensure these ends. Ultimately his authority was absolute. The wife had the responsibility of childbearing and rearing, looking after the domestic side of the home and acting as the authoress of love and affection. The union was enacted on a basis of reciprocal rights and obligations and was seen very much as a contract in which, of course, sexual rights were exclusive to the couple and were used primarily for the sake of procreation.

It is this contractual arrangement of fixed roles that is breaking down extensively in our midst. The evolution of human consciousness reflecting on what is right for human conduct has slowly rejected the authoritarian, privileged position of the husband and has extended considerable rights to the woman, transforming the fixed contract into an open, flexible relationship of equality between the spouses.

Women have yet to achieve full equality in many fields but they have clearly made deep inroads into the inequality of personal relationships in the privacy of their home. The advances in education, provision of work with economic independence and the general climate of opinion is rapidly transforming marriage from a contract to a relationship between complementary equals.

When set roles give way to an intimate relationship no longer governed by fixed rules and regulations, we have on the one hand confusion, of which there is plenty of evidence, and on the other the opportunity to deepen our awareness of the new possibilities that such a situation brings within man's orbit of achievement. It is here I believe that Christianity has a unique responsibility to identify, clarify and spell out what these opportunities are.

Broadly speaking a movement can be discovered in the world to-day which sees the conquest of material deprivation as being a primary objective. The removal of hunger, malnutrition, disease, lack of shelter and and the positive presence of work, housing, employment, health and education are desired goals with which no one will disagree. They have been or are being rapidly achieved in Western societies while the underdeveloped world is struggling with similar aims.

In the West man is searching for something beyond material fulfilment. This can be futile, aimless pleasure seeking – always a risk in times of material success – or a deepening of the image of God in creation through the exploration of a deeper layer of man's potential, namely the psychological, social and instinctual level of fulfilment. I believe this is a legitimate and fully Christian aim which marriage can assist in a way that no other institution can. In my view marriage is a central focal point for man's mastery and deepening of various physical, social and psychological discoveries of our age.

Marriage as a relationship:

When marriage is seen primarily as a relationship and not as a contract, then clearly its survival will depend not so much on forces outside the partners, such as law and children, preserving the bond, but on the ability of the bond to serve their best interests as human beings. In my view the contemporary, monogamous, life-long bond has precisely the ability to achieve this if its characteristics are carefully studied and understood.

Given that marriages will still produce children, even though on average the numbers will be about two to three, the experience of parenthood will remain a vital one and I shall return to this point later but for the time being I would like to concentrate on three other characteristics, namely sustenance, healing and growth which occur in the husband-wife relationship.

Sustaining

No one can survive if the ingredients of security and self-preservation are absent and so it can be taken for granted that a couple must be able to provide these elements for each other. On the positive side one, but increasingly both partners, will go out to work. Work of course provides more than financial advantages. It is a way of reaching others, of strengthening one's identity by creative, purposeful activity. Certainly every couple will in the future consider the possibility that both husband and wife will want to work and share in the advantages of this aspect of life. But for some time to come the wife will expect to be supported, particularly when her children are young. Such activity provides the husband with the opportunity not only of personal advancement at work but also generates many opportunities for sacrifice on behalf of his family.

On the negative side no marriage can survive if one or both partners attack each other physically or psychologically to the point of damage. Physical assaults are easy to recognise and nothing further need be said. Psychological assault is more subtle and it is here that writers like Drs. Laing and Cooper have shown how much ruthless destruction can occur at the psychological level when one member of the family is made the butt of the others, is systematically made the scapegoat and generally treated in a way that invalidates. Their value is questioned, their talents criticized, their worth questioned and they are generally attacked in subtle ways to the point where they lose confidence in themselves or, in the loosest sense of the term, become mad. All of us know of situations where this exists and it is precisely in these homes that marital breakdown can most often be observed.

Healing:

But given that such basic sustenance is maintained, in the past God was thanked for this blessing and not much else was expected. To-day, a good deal more is expected. The opposite of invalidation is *affirmation* and at the psychological level the opportunity of affirmation is uniquely realisable in a contemporary marriage.

The reason for this is that, at the level of interaction, husband and wife are relating on a far more intimate plane than ever before. Previously their interaction was ordained by a distinct predetermined social role which could not be easily modified. But the modification is so extensive nowadays that the encounter between husband and wife will often reach the closeness of the one and only other intimate relationshipship, namely the one between child and parent, particularly child and mother.

It is at this level that the basic human experiences of trust, security, acceptance, receptivity, donation, autonomy, achievement, competence, fear, ambivalence of love and anger, aggression, guilt, repentance and reparation are all learned. Men and women come together in marriage with wounds in all these spheres, some small, others great, which arise either from their specific make-up, their upbringing or a combination of both.

In the intimate experience of marriage there is a second and universal opportunity to heal these wounds in the exchange of love, where one partner can give to the other as far as possible what is missing.

Freud first laid stress on the mechanism of transference. In the psychoanalytic encounter the patient experiences the therapist as a parental figure and relives the appropriate emotions. Transference not only occurs in psychoanalysis but in every sustained close relationship. Modern marriage has precisely the intimacy and closeness which allows each spouse to experience afresh through each other their past and thus be given a new opportunity to receive and learn the missing component from their previous experience. The lessons from psychoanalysis and psychotherapy are the most hopeful and optimistic findings of our age showing man that it is never too late to change provided there is a close, loving, human source from which new experiences can be received and this is the spouse. Christians have always known through their faith that God is endless in his mercy to advance the cause of man and there is plenty of evidence in the Scriptures that marriage is one of his chosen ways to reach humanity. Perhaps in our day we can see more clearly than ever the possibilities of healing in this sacrament.

Through the response of the spouse, both partners can diminish and reverse their fears, the level of their mistrust, the sense of rejection, and their suspiciousness, consequently becoming freer to reveal themselves to others, and receive criticism without feeling destroyed or humiliated. They will also above all, learn for the first time the feeling of being wanted, trusted and appreciated. When this occurs, not only has much healing taken place but, of course, a great deal of growth in the person concerned. That person can now reach out and be reached in a much wider context of life than before, when the world was so threatening and terrifying.

Growth:

But beyond this repairing of wounds which two people can realise for each other, they can also act as agents of personal growth. In the years covered by the phase of marriage such growth is no longer primarily physical or intellectual. By the early twenties the limits of absolute physical and intellectual development have been reached.

As far as the intellect is concerned, however, the full use of the talents of the couple needs a good deal of mutual support. The husband's career can be facilitated by encouragement and even sacrifices made by the wife and the wife's professional or creative potential can greatly be assisted by a co-operative and encouraging husband. In this spirit of give-and-take the firm delineation of the past of the tasks allocated to the partners can be modified and, if necessary, sometimes reversed. When marriage is approached primarily with the aim of achieving the full potential of the members of the family, then life is organised in a mutually facilitating manner rather than pursuing a pre-arranged fixed course.

Work is, of course, a substantial part of the creative growth of an individual: but there are a number of additional or alternative possibilities, such as the pursuit of artistic, literary or other crafts which also need mutual encouragement. Beyond work, however, there lies another area, familiar to psychologists and psychiatrists, of emotional personal growth.

While there are clearly physical and intellectual limits, there are no limits – or at least not measurable ones – of man's psychological differentiation, integration and individuation. The capacity to gain in personal understanding of ourselves has no limits. In this we need someone whom we can trust, with whom we can enter into dialogue, can exchange ideas and emotions, above all, acting as mirrors in which we can see ourselves reflected in ways which would be quite impossible were one alone.

Freud referred to the importance of our unconscious, the part of ourselves which is not open to our consciousness but is open to the observation of others who can help us to see ourselves in ways not otherwise accessible.

The most significant 'other' is, of course, the spouse and, through each other, husband and wife grow deeply in self awareness. They get to know clearly aspects of themselves which they did not know existed at all and recognize the need for a deepening of virtues such as patience, understanding, tolerance, care, concern and compassion. Such growth occurs in the presence of approval when these characteristics are exhibited so that a positive conditioning goes on continuously and is reinforced by the response of the other. Faults are registered but not magnified so that the balance of development is positive.

In this concentrated awareness another human quality emerges, namely that of empathy, which is the ability to feel accurately the inner emotional experiences of another person and respond accurately. All of us start life depending on maternal empathy which acts as a sensitive receiver of the unspoken needs of the speechless child. The desire to be instantly understood and accurately responded to remains with us through life and is one of the clearest expressions of closeness and love between people. Spouses are now able to act in this way as their worlds are separated by as few conventional barriers as possible.

In and through this understanding the ability to respond accurately to others is sharpened and the basis of universal love spreads from our deepening one to one bond to others.

Marriage as the basis for formation of personal bonds:

Critics of marriage will acknowledge these possibilities for healing and growth but will say that they do not need marriage. Any two people coming together who love one another can achieve this. 'We do not need mothers and fathers but mothering and fathering,' writes D. Cooper, one of the severest critics of the family. My answer here is unequivocal. We cannot do without fathers and mothers and so far we have no evidence of any successful alternative. In fact there is increasing ethological evidence to suggest that bond formation in the lower species is widespread.

In man the presence of father and mother – but particularly the latter – provides the baby with the unique opportunity to form a whole series of personal attachments to her. The child has in-built capacities to look at mother's face, smile , touch, hold, explore, make distress calls, laugh and play. If we care to think, many of our adult anger appeasement actions are directly related to these experiences of love we first had with our mother. We greet the stranger, who then ceases to be one, smile at the anonymous person with whom personal contact has now been made, befriend those we offer food to and share a meal with, are moved to compassion in the presence of anything small, helpless, childlike and our anger is mitigated when another person assumes a diminutive stance.

The mother, and later father-child, relationship is not only the means of the unique bond formation of love but it is also the essential biological infrastructure for love and peace with others.

But this bond formation cannot occur with random strangers. It needs a continuous, reliable and predictable relationship. We certainly need mothers and fathers for only they can provide these conditions.

And so with marriage which is the second and only other intimate experience. It too needs the condition of continuity, reliability and predictability within which sustaining, healing and growth can take place. Here lies the strongest answer to promiscuous behaviour which interrupts the link between sex and the possibility of the development of personal links.

Christianity does not need to apologize for its absolute conviction that the central teaching of Christ on marriage is as relevant and true to-day as it has ever been in the history of man. But its characteristics have changed enormously and it is our task to understand this and prepare the next generation adequately. We have much to give to others by a renewal of our understanding of marriage and the family as the basic structure through which the foundations of love are established.

But for committed Christians marriage means much more. In the family men, women and children recognize and learn the meaning of love, children from their parents, parents deepening it through each other. Whenever love is encountered, there the nature of God is most closely perceived. Marriage has been defined as a sacrament by the Roman Catholic Church and there is much in the Anglican tradition which can recognize and identify with the essence of this teaching even if it disagrees on the details. I sincerely hope that one feature of ecumenism will be the convergence by all Christian Churches on this sacrament which is the precious inheritance of all.

For ultimately this sacrament of interpersonal communication teaches us and prepares for the meaning of love in Eternity. Every time a husband or a wife separate from each other for an hour, a day or more they carry within themselves, internalise, the other. In the absence of sight, touch and vision, love is retained and now no longer needs the immediacy of physical contact for its experience. This is the nearest understanding of love in eternity, at least until the resurrection of the body, but even then we are told by Christ there will be no taking in marriage in heaven. But if marriage is the institution for the establishment of bonds of love then its uniqueness for preparing us for this, in this world and eschatologically, is second to none.

Thus Christianity, far from being on the defensive about the essentials of marriage, can contemplate the future with alacrity for a new era is opening in which the Christian ideals of personal growth in love will have a greater opportunity than ever before of being realized.

MARRIAGE AND THE SINGLE STATE I

As a strong advocate both of marriage and the single state dedicated to God, my position has appeared to some contradictory. In particular the question has been raised whether — in the light of modern knowledge — the single state can be considered compatible with full human development and, if the answer is in the negative, is the Church's insistence on this state a violation of human integrity?

I shall not attempt to answer this question in detail but let me state instead that I am fully committed to the view that in the single state the Catholic Church has a precious tradition that needs preserving. In order, however, to preserve and strengthen it, we need a fundamental and radical reappraisal of the meaning both of marriage and of the single state because the two are intimately related. On this occasion I shall concentrate on marriage primarily and briefly compare the single state with it at some points and then consider subsequently areas of practical co-operation between the two.

Marriage is a sacrament and a sacrament is a permanent sign of grace, established by Christ and efficacious *ex opere operato*. This precise theological language leaves all, except the trained theologian, utterly mystified and needs elucidation to grasp its richness.

Ultimately the sign that Christians are concerned with is that of the Trinitarian God, the second person of which, Jesus Christ, revealed himself in the Incarnation, living, dying and rising again for us. Christ is the visible sign of the unseen God and the Church, composed of all the faithful, is the continuation of this sign. It is the visible manifestation of his Body. The transformation of the individual into a Christian depends on uniting with and relating to Christ. The Church as a whole and the seven sacraments in particular allow us to do precisely this. A sacrament is, therefore, a meeting point between each one of us and Christ and it is this meeting, this encounter, for which the Church exists and which gives meaning to all that she does. At a time of unprecedented confusion, conflict amd painful acrimony, it is worth reminding ourselves that this is what the Church's responsibility is, and everything else, particularly personal animosities and rancour, must be subordinated to this unique task of making Christ increasingly clear to the world.

We become members of this mystical body by baptism, we are revitalised at the Holy Eucharist and more than ninety per cent of

Christians encounter Christ most intimately and continuously in the sacrament of marriage. It is my personal conviction that one way by which the Church will bring Christ back most effectively into the world — which is its mission — is through a renewal of the meaning of marriage and in this task it will need the co-operation, understanding and help of the single person dedicated to God. To accomplish this what is needed is an on-going re-examination of the meaning of marriage in contemporary terms. In a variety of publications I have attempted to indicate that one of the clearest ways of understanding this change is the shift away from seeing this sacrament merely as a contract to that of a relationship which is in keeping most accurately with its description in the Scriptures and its living reality amongst the married. It is not possible to go over this ground here but instead I would like to examine contemporary marriage in the light of its many profound changes and how these affect our traditional Christian image of this sacrament.

Vatican II calls marriage a 'community of love' and this succinct but magnificent phrase is the starting point of all understanding of marriage. A community is made up of interacting persons and love is the distillate of this communication expressed socially, physically, psychologically and spiritually.

Marriage itself brings about the formation of the unit composed of husband, wife and children, the so-called nuclear family, living frequently at a distance from the family of origin as opposed to the past when grandparents, married sons and daughters and their children lived in one extended household. This separation, coupled with urbanization and a much greater frequency of change of work, has thrown the nuclear family very much more on its own resources and one of the principal challenges of Christianity is the fostering of a genuine and loving community which can contribute towards the breakdown of isolation, the reduction of loneliness, facilitating interaction and, wherever necessary, providing support in those instances where the family cannot cope. In the middle of this flux and confusion, the single person provides the vital continuity and availability of establishing the community and links within it out of the disparate, socially mobile and often transient membership. Education and preparation for this must surely form one of the key features of the training for the priesthood and religious life, depending heavily on the insights of sociology and psychology.

Returning to the nuclear marriage, the newly weds are getting to know each other. Sociologists will describe in this early phase the clarification of roles, namely which spouse assumes what responsibility and agreement on how the house should be run. In the absence of rigidly adhered socially sanctioned roles, the couple need to establish their own pattern. If the wife is working, then the clearly delineated task of housekeeping allocated to her in the past will have to be shared and her economic independence at this stage will give her power hitherto confined to the man.

But beyond this social reconnaissance, the couple will be discovering each other physically in their bodily and sexual communication. Here Christianity has the urgent task of revaluing human sexuality. This is a huge topic but some points need emphasising repeatedly.

The first one is the fact that until very recently Christian thinking on sex tied it extensively with procreation, beautifully summarised in Vatican II in the following sentence: 'By their very nature, the institution of matrimony itself and conjugal love are ordained for the procreation and education of children and find in them their ultimate crown.' But later on the statement makes it clear that 'Marriage to be sure is not instituted solely for procreation.' The separation of sex from procreation is a focal point of development in the twentieth century and lies at the heart of many head-on clashes between Christianity and humanism.

A little more care with the facts and little less of undisciplined, emotional outbursts could clarify many of the problems. First of all the design of the creator, clearly shown in the sexual physiology of the woman, shows that procreation for the average woman is only possible over a short time, twenty-four to seventy-two hours each month. Secondly the advent of birth regulation has brought even this limited span far more under man's control. Thirdly, this century has seen a critical point in the history of mankind whereby overpopulation and not failure to reproduce threatens it with extinction. Such startling changes have caught Christianity and much of society completely unprepared.

Furthermore, the advent of modern medicine has made reproduction a much safer process. Thus the combination of all these factors has tended to reduce the size of the family, to bring child bearing to a close much earlier – on an average the late twenties – and, in combination with the longer duration of marriage, leaves an unprecedented period of sexual communication disconnected with procreation as such.

This means that sexual intercourse has to be understood overwhelmingly other than in its procreative potential and for this we need an exclusively psychological approach. It also helps to compare the difference in human relationship where it is present, as in marriage, and where it is absent, as in the single state.

Whenever sexual intercourse was considered in the past, two of its characteristics held precedence. These were its capability to give instinctual pleasure and to procreate. Christianity, full of apprehension about sexual pleasure, reduced its significance to procreation. Freud, on the other hand, elevated instinct as the fundamental basis for the development of the personality. Both have been seriously wrong but Christianity is more culpable for it failed to grasp the obvious, namely that the physical, the body, is capable of expressing something infinitely more, namely it is the means by which we communicate some of the most precious human qualities of love.

Modern psychology has clearly shown how our earliest and most significant experiences were received in our first few years of life when physical contact was one of the principal means of conveying the feeling of recognition, closeness, acceptance, trust and security. We received all these feelings in the arms and on the knees of our parents. Physical touch was the principal way of communicating these feelings. Freud called all of this infantile sexuality. The nomenclature is immaterial, the facts are inescapable. On each occasion when two people touch each other, they are capable of confining the experience to an instinctual, erotic level; they are also capable of experiencing through the body the feelings of recognition, acceptance, trust, care, concern, forgiveness and reconciliation – in short, of love. This is precisely how human sexuality functions in marriage, whereby the instinctual is the channel, the means by which the couple reach each other, affirm and reaffirm their significance for one another in a continuous relationship. Whenever the instinctual is separated from the affectionate and the promotion of personal contact, there is a severe restriction of its human potential and this introduces the basic sense of immorality in human sexuality. In the presence of a relationship of integrity which is usually, but not necessarily, present in marriage, the sexual pleasure is a powerful vehicle for the sustaining, healing and growth of the couple.

This sustaining, healing and growth of the human person needs to go on just as much in the single person and a person entering the single state must possess characteristics in their personality which can compensate for the absence of an exclusive one-to-one relationship with its powerful capacity for sexual renewal. This means that single people far from denying their sexuality – whatever its intensity – accept it and make it a part if their conscious self. They are fully men and women and certainly do not embrace the single state to escape from sexuality. There is no place in this state for those who are afraid of being fully human and, to the extent that the single state attracted or made it possible to harbour such people, it fell short of its full meaning, which is the richness of the personality of the second person of the Trinity. On the contrary, the single person must possess this capacity for complete growth from the moment he enters the religious life, or at least have abilities which will develop later, permitting him to develop relations with other people similar to those of his married brothers and sisters, without, of course, any exclusive one-to-one sexual encounter.

69

If this view is accepted, it will have a radical impact on the type of person who is selected for this vocation. Both married and single are responding to God the Father through Christ with the assistance of the Spirit. This response is one which aims at the richest possible realization of their humanity. This much is common to all. The overwhelming majority need marriage and sexual communion, a few have the gifts which dispense with this but both are aiming at the fullest possible growth of the image of God in them and both require relationship as the means of achieving this. The central crisis in religious life is to grasp this truth and to restructure community life to bring about this closeness and intimacy which can generate sustaining, healing and growth without the exclusive sexual relationship of marriage. Nothing else will suffice because the witness of love must stem from a continuous renewal and growth of love which is based on relationship with God and neighbour. Possibly the greatest tragedy in the sacrament of marriage is the encounter of the spouses, meeting Christ in each other, the source of all love, and yet being incapable of experiencing, giving and receiving this quality of love. Whenever this occurs, there is no marriage. Possibly the greatest tragedy in the single state dedicated to God is the so-called encounter with God, with Christ, the source of all love, through prayer, sacraments and in community life, when such a person is incapable of sustaining relationships of love with other human beings. Both situations are contradictions and unbeknown to us have been fostered both in marriage and the single state by concentrating on convincing impersonal substitutes such as law, authority and empty ritual.

Given the significance of the sexual act in terms of its capacity to foster and maintain the relationship, does this mean that children are now to be relegated to the fringe of married life? Not at all. Instead their education, the quality of child rearing, becomes the first priority. It is not quantity but quality that matters now and not quality merely in material and educational terms. There are parts of the world and pockets in our country where poverty in terms of food, shelter and disease is still rampant and educational facilities poor or absent. But in the developed countries much of this is assumed to be present. In its presence, attention needs to shift to the growth of the personality. In the past it was taken for granted that sending a child to a Catholic school was sufficient in itself. We have learned that this is not enough. Apart from the arguments about Catholic schools and their purpose, everyone now recognizes that the school which is not supported by the home is seriously weakened in its work. At home what is needed is a viable, flourishing and loving husband-wife relationship which will meet the growing needs of the children.

If the parents are to recognize and meet the needs of their children, they must recognize and meet each other's needs. At the social level there is a growing desire for openness, freedom and equality which are the basic conditions within which love at a personal level can be expressed. What does such personal expression imply? Here the psychological sciences – particularly psychoanalysis – have shown that, as a relationship increases in intimacy losing the fixed, social, impersonal character, so it returns to the direct encounter which characterized the first ever relationship, namely that between parents and children. In other words, adults – and that means husband and wife – need similar experiences from each other as they received in their first and only other intimate relationship in life, namely their childhood.

Certain features of the child-parent relationship which are repeated in the husband-wife one are essential for the viability and stability of marriage without which there can be no marriage. The first is trust. The basic quality that each child requires for survival is to place his trust in parents whom he knows will provide a continuous, reliable and predictable relationship, which takes care of his physical, emotional and social requirements. It is out of this nourishing sustaining of childhood that the nature of trust in others is established. Hence it is also the basis for trust in the Divine Other. Without trust, human relationships crumble. Spouses need to continue to offer this increasingly to each other. The Christ-Church imagery of marriage fits in beautifully with the generation and sustaining of trust.

Within this trust, the child learns to feel recognized, wanted and appreciated as a unique person. This uniqueness will be distributed in various characteristics of intelligence, temperament and physique with the millions of combinations which make every person a distinct entity. This need to feel affirmed and confirmed as a person does not cease in childhood; it goes on throughout life and spouses act as the most powerful affirming and confirming agents for each other.

Beyond this affirmation, the child learns the pangs of conflict, competition, envy, jealousy and hostility from which spring the horrors of rejection, damage and destructiveness. The child can be confirmed, it can also be repudiated: spouses can affirm, they can also repudiate, reject and slowly destroy each other. Human relationships emerge out of this mixture of love and frustration, anger and reconciliation and love is the characteristic we assign to all behaviour that affirms, heals and promotes growth and the spouses, in loving one another, meet Christ, the source of all love.

But such love is not confined to marriage. The single require it as well and it is life in community that provides the structure within which this love will be realised. Community life, like marriage, is also abandoning its distant, impersonal, rigid character and you all know the tensions and suffering this implies.

But for married and single the faith which we profess finds its most

71

authentic realisation in the love of our neighbour. For the married the most precious neighbour is husband or wife: for the single person the others in the community. From these respective communities of family and religious life we prepare ourselves to reach others, our children, friends, and those we serve. We cannot really love others unless we learn how to love those close to us and through each other continue to renew our own love for ourselves.

In this new type of marriage the quality of the relationship will become increasingly crucial. The parents who are able to trust, affirm and confirm each other will in turn give to their children the foundations of trust, independence, self-assurance, self-directing, self-determination, in short of self acceptance. It is out of the ranks of such self-accepting, secure personalities, people who have tasted the meaning of love in their homes, that the recruits of the next generation of single people dedicated to God will emerge: people with different characteristics but carrying on the tradition of serving Christ.

The Spiritual

The meaning of the spiritual in marriage is now a little clearer. The Catholic Church has declared marriage to be a sacrament and to-day we can see the immense significance of this teaching a little more clearly. As the nature of marriage changes, the spouses and their children relate to each other in an ever deeper and wider context of social, physical and emotional encounter. As the involvement extends, it engages far more of the humanity of the interacting members. The greater the engagement the nearer is the approximation of the members of each family to the image of God. Far from decrying the fullness of the exchange which is extending beyond intellect and will into the world of feelings and instincts, we have, through marriage, the possibility of getting a little more insight into the depths of the divine mystery of the Trinity. The husband-wife relationship has been used by St. Paul as a symbol for the relationship between Christ and the Church and in turn through Christ as an avenue to the mystery of God. This sacrament is one vital gateway for understanding the nature of God, always remembering the difference between the Creator and the created but remembering also that in and through the Incarnation we have become adopted children of the Father and are therefore capable of sharing in this Divine life here and now. The relationship between husband and wife is a vivid encounter with Christ for two people as individuals, but the collective evolution of marriage unfolds a richer understanding of the mystery of God as spouses reflect the divine image in their increasingly penetrating encounter with each other.

MARRIAGE AND THE SINGLE STATE II

The most convenient point to start this section is to state categorically that what is needed above all for marriage is education for this sacrament. It is no exaggeration to state that the training preparation for this vital vocation has been lamentably inadequate. The little that was available consisted of sexual prohibitions before and within marriage and the instructions regarding the fulfilment of the legal requirements for the ceremony. Briefly what every Catholic was taught was to avoid occasions of sex in courtship, marry – if at all possible – a fellow Catholic, in a Catholic Church in the prescribed way, avoid the use of birth control afterwards and send their children to a Catholic school. There is a lot of wisdom in these instructions but by no stretch of the imagination can they be considered the essentials for ensuring stable, life-long relationships of love. The evidence for this is precisely the number of Catholics who followed this advice faithfully, resorted to prayer and the sacraments as well, only to find that their marriage still broke down. It may be argued that without these instructions many more marriages would have broken down. This is something that cannot be proved but whether it is true or not, it is abundantly clear to-day that a community of love needs preparation for a personal relationship and therefore the emphasis has to shift emphatically to a continuous education to prepare people to initiate and sustain such a partnership spanning many decades, perhaps fifty years or more.

Such an education starts from the cradle onwards and the first focus of attention must be the parents who have to educate their children. Education here implies far more than intellectual and social training, although these form an essential background. What each child needs is to receive an appropriate response from the parents at each stage of its development. Scores of books have been written describing the social, intellectual and psychological development of children. There is no need for parents to possess degrees in these behavioural sciences in order to be good parents. What is needed is a sensitive awareness of the child's unique requirements and a sympathetic response to them. Most of it is intuitive but a great deal more can be achieved if parents can meet to discuss and learn from each other. Here several practical points emerge. A parish priest, a nun or, preferably, a parish team should ensure that no parish exists in Britain which does not have a variety of family groups operating. It should be part of the responsibility of every

Catholic school to ensure that the parents of the children attending are offered this opportunity. Organising and sustaining such groups is no easy task. Parents come together and then depart as their requirements change. It is the priest or the religious, in co-operation with the laity, who can function as the continuity and co-ordinating link. Secondly such groups need material and leadership. There is a growing range of suitable books, some provided by the Catholic Marriage Guidance Council and by other agencies. It would be the responsibility of the organising group to ensure that the material is up to date and available. When the occasion arises a group might feel its experiences are worth putting in print.

It should be emphasised that the role of the nun or priest is not to spoon feed the faithful. The time is past for such pastoral activity and it should be discouraged. What is needed is the presence of a continuous catalytical action. So much never happens in a parish because of the absence of a source of continuity which is aware of the needs of people. The erection and maintenance of family groups supporting parents is an absolute necessity for the future of the Christian community and will, of course meet different needs depending of the social group concerned.

Perhaps in a sophisticated community what is needed is the opportunity to discuss at length and in depth the emotional development of the child and its sexual education and in another simply for parents to come together and share their common experiences. What our contemporary society requires is the possibility for parents to turn to each other, breaking the sense of loneliness and isolation that the urbanized communities foster. The extended family of the past, which provided support through the presence of grandparents and other relatives in the immediate neighbourhood, needs to be replaced by the spontaneous and renewed formation of groups of people with common interests.

The support that the nun can give does not stop there. The possibilities are endless. In some areas, particularly in the cities and towns, the worst features of contemporary life are the isolation and lack of help that is often to be found. There may be a need to establish something far more adventurous, such as a continuous telephone service manned twenty four hours a day by nuns to whom any distressed household can ring for help and advice. There are increasingly organisations like the Samaritans and good neighbour schemes such as Care which aim to provide emergency relief in desperate situations. There is no reason why the Christian community cannot get together and instigate a twenty-four hour telephone service to which a mother, newly arrived in the district and struck down with illness, or an elderly, lonely person needing help, can appeal. The person answering the call will then put them in contact with whatever statutory or voluntary services exist in the community to relieve the immediate distress. A service like that will bring married and single together in a unique way as each responds to the other with the least delay and the maximum of efficiency. Such a service would require a team of women and men, religious and lay, available on a rota with a telephone number which is known to the parish. In an emergency parishioners can turn for help and be assured of a willing response. At the manning point there should be comprehensive information about the voluntary organisations that can aid. Such a scheme might well be shared by other Christian communities. The possibility of the nun going into a home and helping with baby sitting in times of illness or crisis is something that is already occurring here and there and could easily be extended if the personnel were available.

Both these approaches will help to break down some of the traditions of the past which kept the nun behind the security of her convent walls and only brought her into contact with her fellow Christians in formal settings such as school, hospital, orphanage when she offered her services in a clearly defined context. This inevitably created a distance between her and her fellow Christians, perpetuating the "we" and "they" situation. Similarly the priest met his parishioners in a fixed role which demanded service but which was transacted with a mutually agreed aloofness rarely penetrated. The people met him at formal times in the liturgy, at social functions and when he was visiting or help was sought. But in all these situations there were clear cut roles acted out which maintained the "we" and "they" position and it was certainly the exceptional priest who shared and understood the intimate, emotional, inner life of the family. Increasingly this restricted and rigid approach needs to give way to a flexible, informal, and in some ways, infinitely more generous exchange as priest and people encounter each other spontaneously without the restrictions of the past.

Education continues at school from about five to late teens and preparation for marriage needs to become a central feature of this programme. At the present moment education for marriage is beginning to develop with the initiation of Catholic Marriage Advisory Council personnel who come to school on single or extended occasions and, with or without the assistance of staff, make their contribution. Invaluable as this is at this inaugural stage, it needs large scale extension. Education for marriage must become part of a total approach to the possibilities of human relationship, which every school must consider essential to the education of children. Such a programme will need the corporate effort of all the staff with allocation of special responsibility to individual members who are suited for this work. Preparation for such work must reflect appropriate training courses in Teacher Training colleges and postgraduate programmes. Here is an area which needs urgent expansion in planning, research and experimentation. If the Christian community is to continue to justify its Christian schools, then one of its unique contributions must be the preparation of men and women who are able to comprehend and respond to the complex human situation of our day. This means becoming aware of the authentic trends towards openness, frankness, realisation of potential, attention to the emotional side of man, to equality of the sexes, to responsible decision making based on equality and inner directness and, above all, to a comprehension of love in to-day's world. These features stand in contradiction to the rigidity, fixity and, as far as marriage and sexuality are concerned, the sheer ignorance and irrelevance of the recent past.

It hardly needs saying that Christianity has the unique opportunity of reversing the disastrous policy of the last twenty-five years and replacing sexual education by education for marriage. Instead of spending endless hours discussing whether this or that sex film is suitable, the Christian community should take the initiative and prepare men and women for marriage, within which human sexuality will be encountered in all its fullness. But the success of marriage as a relationship will depend on the capacity of people to understand themselves and their spouse accurately, to learn how to express their feelings to one another, to adapt traditional marriage patterns, so that the wife can have a much wider choice of activity as far as work is concerned, without sacrificing the essential requirements of her children. Here the Christian schools can give a special lead by making provisions for the return to teaching of married women on a part time basis a special feature, if necessary backed by the provision of creches.

Such women could assume the special responsibility for the education programme for preparation of marriage. Such a programme would need to focus on the characteristics of the human personality at all stages but particularly from puberty onwards and stress how the man-woman relationship helps to sustain, heal and promote personal growth. Here special attention will be needed to go beyond the social characteristics of dress, language, recreation, work and into the psychological ones of relationship on the basis of trust, reassurance, security, self confidence, acceptance, rejection, conflict, realization of potential, dependence, independence, initiative, fear, anxiety, guilt, tension and its relief and all the other essential ingredients without which education is so markedly defective. The terrible price that is being paid in human casualties in contemporary society is only likely to be reversed when our education alters course from a social and intellectual training to a total personality training in which the affective and psychological side of man receives an equivalent or even greater amount of attention than the other two. We have suffered the illusion that this was adequately catered for in our religious training. To the extent that this consisted of a series of do's and don'ts it certainly gave helpful guide lines but in no sense could it be considered the ideal. It imposed a partly digested external framework of discipline which frequently broke down as the experience of the inner person could not understand or use the code of discipline. There could either be blind obedience to external authority, the ideal up to now, or total abandonment as the prescription of authority became irrelevant to the exigencies of life. Much of Christianity has been rejected, not because it has been found wanting, but because a poorly comprehended, externally imposed discipline has appeared meaningless. This is not to say that authority and discipline are no longer required. Far from it. What is needed is an education that really reaches the inner experience of human beings so that the morality they are taught reflects sensitively and accurately things as they really are. Christian marriage as lived and the teaching received for it at school have been truly worlds apart and, since it is within marriage and the family that many of the significant transactions of life occur, preparation for Christian life has been sadly deficient.

There are some specific points that need highlighting. Every piece of research has shown that youthful marriages are extremely vulnerable. Marriges under twenty carry a high risk of breakdown. Incidentally, admission to religious life from this age group also carries a high incidence of breakdown. There is, of course, a common factor; namely that in both instances people change markedly so that the psychological needs which prompted them to seek the security of a partner or that of religious life are no longer operating so powerfully years later when they discover that their husband or wife, or religious life has become incomprehensible, a stranger to their developed selves.

One way of avoiding these tragedies is first of all to focus fully on this danger. We have multiple training programmes; we need an equally extensive one for marriage in which certain risks are repeatedly spelled out annually, starting from eleven or twelve onwards, as part of the on-going teaching. But it is not enough to warn; we have to help people to negotiate the pressures which lead to these hasty unions. Psychologically two factors are relevant. First of all, loneliness and secondly, the crisis in identity. 'Who am I?' is the repeated, undeclared cry of so many adolescents. With a ring on their hand, such a person has a status, role and identity; thanks to a ceremony and the blessing of the Church one has become a wife or a husband. But ceremonies and rituals do not give confidence, understanding, security, knowledge and before long such a person is confused and lost, once again, because the role of wife or husband is no substitute for personal growth.

Here is a vast challenge in helping young people to find companionship and meaning to life, other than by living together to reduce their problems. If they do get married, such a couple need extra help in finding a house and, if the wife has got a young child, much support so that some of her time is freed to attend to her husband. Here the nun is in an excellent position to reach and help such couples by baby sitting or bringing them in touch with other couples similarly placed so that a self-helping community can emerge. Our first urgent need is to identify such vulnerable couples. Much can be done if the community learns to recognise and respond to the danger signals in time.

At present such preparation for marriage as is taking place tends to stress the pre-nuptial period with courses for engaged couples. These are most useful but education for marriage is a continuing process and, as matrimony goes through various phases, what is required is a continuous matching programme of education. This can be done in at least two ways.

Firstly we need a radical change in the liturgical and spiritual framework within which marriage is experienced. If we look at the Scriptures, there is ample material to deal with the experience of the family at all stages of its development. There is no reason why the marrying cycle of dating, courtship, engagement, marriage, arrival of first child, arrival of subsequent children, departure of children to school, puberty, adolescence, departure of children from home, change of life and other important events such as sickness and bereavement in the marriage cycle should not be linked with scriptural passages and prayers which will form a whole new approach, linking the experience of the sacrament with prayer, discussion and meditation both at home and at church. There is an urgent need for such a development which once again will bring the single person and the married together in a unique way. There is no need to abolish the single state in order to enrich the understanding of marriage by the single. But such a development will remain another pious hope unless practical and imaginative steps are taken to bring the two together. Such a development could also break down the cynicism whereby people only make contact with the Church at their baptism, their wedding and their funeral.

The second step requires the formation of discussion groups among the married themselves, not to consider their children but their own experience of marriage. Such an idea fills some with horror but such an anxiety is unjustified. Such discussions goes on unceasingly over the wall, in the factory, in the office, in the pub as men and women seek understanding and reassurance about their sexual life or other intimate aspects of marriage. It is a huge pretence on the part of the Christian community to suggest that such delicate issues should not be discussed publicly. It did not stop St. Paul considering such issues in his epistle to the Corinthians. Christianity can encourage and structure such exchanges and help people to a truer and deeper understanding of themselves.

In such encounters the single person will come into close contact with the married. Reference has been made to the transactions in the past which brought the two together but there remained an essential aloofness between them, principally because their inner worlds were not meeting. The great change that is occurring in the relationship between the priest, the nun, and the people of God is the development, admittedly slow, painful and acrimonious, in the nature of this exchange. In the past the single person dedicated to God was seen as, and experienced himself or herself as, part of an authoritarian structure that responded by directing, giving advice and instruction. When it came to marriage, there were a number of rules and instructions that could be and were given in practice with a mixture of care, compassion, understanding and sympathy.

To-day the Church is slowly moving away from this fixed exchange. This alteration is the source of the most widespread conflict and anxiety. Essentially the eternal truths remain unchanged but the response of the people of God is no longer that of passive, submissive, receiving pupils. The exchange is frank, open, not didactic; statements are challenged and people want to be infinitely more personally responsible and inner directed in their ultimate actions. For some, this spells chaos, anarchy and the end of the Catholic Church. The Church on the other hand has decided to move in this direction and, if faith means anything, it requires trust in the operation of the Spirit at this moment of change.

As far as marriage is concerned, such a change means that the single do not need to approach it with the anxiety that, having no intimate experience of the state, they are not equipped to enter into a meaningful relationship with those who have. They need not worry that, having exhausted the theological answers, their contribution ceases. In the developing new relationship, frequently they will not be asked to give advice and, if they are, they should be careful before doing so. Instead they will be approached as people who have concern, patience and interest to enter into a discussion. This will allow the married person to look into the situation afresh in a frank encounter between two human beings. Both will bring their humanity into the exchange, imbued with Christian love. The married person will focus on his or her personality and out of the exchange some new insight will emerge, perhaps not on the first occasion but over a period of time. Careful listening, avoidance of a judgemental approach, patience and genuine loving response are the ingredients with which married and single will meet each other in the future. They will share their humanity which will be particularised in different ways but they will be no longer

79

strangers, communicating indirectly through a set of rules and instructions which governed the exchange in the past, and which ran the risk of creating a dialogue of the deaf. This does not mean that rules and regulations have disappeared. What it does mean is that the greater part of life cannot be lived by law but only by love, which is the principal law, translated into a myriad of detailed individual responses.

The presence of the single person dedicated to God will bring to the married the living reality of a man or woman instructed in Christian principles but, above all, aware of the effort and suffering that is needed to practise them. They will bring much more than detailed instruction. Rather through their life they will offer the living evidence of sustained hope, encouragement, conviction and determination that what both single and married care for, namely Christ, is a realisable reality. The married in turn will bring to the single person the living evidence that loving Christ in their spouse and children is the daily drama within which a substantial part of Christian life is lived. The encounter will strengthen and comfort both by moving determinedly away from the characteristics that differentiate and separate them, so often stressed in the past, to the features that they share. This is their common humanity, lived out in joy, sorrow, fear, uncertainty, sharing one central feature, an intense awareness and desire to meet and live with Christ in their daily activity, a reality that will unite all in the life of resurrection where marriage will not exist but personal relationships of love will triumph.

THE SINGLE STATE, COMMUNITY AND PERFECTION

In the last ten years the Church has experienced an unprecedented degree of unrest and confusion which is bound to continue for some time to come. This was inevitable if the task of recognising and experiencing Christ, and through Christ, and Father and the Spirit, is to be accomplished meaningfully in our age.

The word 'meaningful' is an overworked one and it is essential to clarify the particular point at issue. The issue that concerns everyone is the search for the truth in a way which identifies the need for change, if necessary radical change, without destroying any aspect of a precious heritage which truly reflects and embodies the continuing presence of the Incarnation in the world.

One such area of marked confusion is that of sexuality, marriage and the single state. Christianity has to be particularly sensitive in this domain for two reasons. The first is that it is in the bosom — and only in the bosom — of Christianity that sexuality and love truly fuse. The second is that for some very complicated reason Christianity has been unable hitherto to do full justice to the richness of this precious gift of God and as a result many, far too many, people have dismissed the likelihood of the Christian voice having anything useful to say on this subject.

For over a decade now I have been trying to explore afresh the richness of Christianity in this area and in the process have inevitably had to face the central question whether the single state dedicated to God can still be regarded as truly representing an authentic part of Christ's voice in the world to-day. In answering this vital question I have been privileged to talk and listen to scores of religious in a variety of personal predicaments, ranging from the urgent desire to leave their single state to the most serene and reassuring acceptance of it.

For one who eulogises the significance of marriage and the sexual life it might be expected that I would join the growing chorus of voices that question the validity of celibacy. Let me state emphatically that the longer I reflect on its meaning the more convinced I become of its vital part in the life of the Christian community. But like so much else centuries of stagnation have led to such pressures for practical changes that there is a real danger of ignoring the need for radical reformulation of the meaning of the single state dedicated to God.

In this address I shall not be concerned about such details as the

81

type of dress to be worn, the social habits pertaining to drinking, smoking, entertainments that are considered respectable, hours of returning to the community, etc. In my view these are topics about which much time can be wasted without touching the heart of the matter. Any reference to these or other details will be related to an examination of the inner life of the single person which I consider the central issue and which will be examined through the background of my psychological understanding of the nature of being human. The nearer we get to an understanding of human nature, the closer we get to the image of God reflected in man and one of the growing foci of theological awareness is that a theology, which is isolated from the behaviour sciences of sociology, psychology, anthropology, cannot any longer do justice to the truth with which it is attempting to grapple.

With this in mind, it is worth considering afresh a crucial notion for all Christian life, but in particular that of the single person. Incidentally, in relating the special instance of the single person to all Christian life, I am drawing attention to the artificial separation that has existed in the past between those who, in the eyes of many, were characterised by the things they could not do − such as marrying, having material things or ordinary clothes − and the rest who could do these things. This separation or emphasis, whose superficial details are still insisted upon as the real marks of significance, is utterly false. The single and the married share a common Christian life and the married are as much committed to the life of perfection as the single. What really matters is not the surface distinctions, the denials and the apparent deprivations of the religious life but the attainment of fullness in and through Jesus Christ.

Fullness and Emptiness:

Central to this is the meaning of fullness and emptiness in Christian life specially referred to in the decree on the Religious Life.

"The fact that they are in God's service should ignite and fan within them the exercise of virtue, especially humility, obedience, courage and chastity. Through them they share spiritually in Christ's self surrender. (cf. Phil. 2: 7-8) and in His life: (cf. Rom. 8: 1-13).

The reference to Philippians is important and St. Paul should be quoted. Writing to the Church at Philippi from prison, he exhorts them to be Christlike.

'In your minds you must be the same as Christ Jesus:
His state was divine
Yet he did not cling

to his equality with God
but emptied himself
to assume the condition of a slave
and became as men are
he was humbler yet
even to accepting death,
death on the cross.'

Philip 2: 5-8

Here, as everywhere in the New Testament, we are confronted either with the most momentous fact, namely that God chose of his own free will to become man and thus allows us here and now to share in his Divine fullness as an anticipation of that sharing for all eternity, or a glaring collective illusion and deception, neither God nor Christ remotely reflecting the reality we attach to them. Faith is the deciding element in the variety of interpretations. But, having made the personal decision, it is vital that our lives illuminate the truth we believe in so that others may see it too. It is when others cannot see Christ in us that the Church needs to worry. The withdrawal from Christ has been proceeding at an accelerating rate for a long time. Through a process of massive denial, the Church did not realise that this was not due to the blindness and obstinacy of others but rather to the failure to do justice to the precious truths we possess. Thank God that period is now over. A renewed interest in the Scriptures and an examination of man's deepening understanding of himself through the behavioural and biological sciences have become two invaluable tools of renewal. Both impinge on deeply ingrained patterns of thought and behaviour which are not easy to alter; hence the continuing tension in the ensuing dialogue.

St. Paul and the Church urge us to follow Christ in emptying ourselves and, as I know only too well, this is precisely the reason given by many people for actually leaving the religious life. What has gone wrong? Are these women and men truly lacking in Christian understanding, generosity and love which are sometimes the insensitive labels attached to them by those who find their behaviour a repudiation of commitment to faith and to their vows?

I have met several of these people and some of them are the most caring, generous and loving persons the Christian community could wish to have. This is not to imply that only those who depart have these characteristics; far from it. Many who remain are equally rich. At this point I could pursue the reasons for this difference in behaviour but that is not the object of this paper.

What both groups share is a sense of, an awareness of, personal maturity which they wish to put at the disposal of God, although in different ways. And it is this sense of personal fullness, possession of self, perfection to which I wish to draw attention. All references to Christ's emptying himself can only be correctly interpreted if understood in terms of Christ's fullness, completion, the full possession of himself. He could not give up what he did not possess and St. Paul makes this perfectly clear elsewhere.

In his letter to the Church at Colossae he describes Christ in these words:
'He is the image of the unseen God
and the first-born of all creation,
for in him were created all things in
heaven and on earth.
Everything visible and everything invisible,
Thrones, Dominations, Sovereignties, Powers
All things were created through him and for him.
Before anything was created, he existed,
And he holds all things in unity.
Now the Church is his body,
He is its head.

As he is in the Beginning,
He was first to be born from the dead,
so that he should be first in every way
because God wanted all perfection
to be found in him.'

Col: 1: 15-19

The word perfection is translated elsewhere as fullness, in other words, a complete possession of self. Christ is the model of such 'self-possession' and it was this which enabled him freely to sacrifice 'self', in and through love, for the sake of humanity.

'The Father loves me,
because I lay down my life
in order to take it up again,
No one takes it from me;
I lay it down of my own free will.'

John 10: 18

The Christian who gives up anything to God or his neighbour must first possess it and the whole Christian tradition, particularly exemplified in the single state, which has singled out the sacrificial in imitating Christ, can only reflect accurately the donation if it preserves and promotes accurately this plenitude. One of the central points of

84

crisis in Christianity to-day is its inability to convince the world that it knows how to promote the fullness of the person which is the legitimate aspiration of contemporary man.

If religious life has the validity I believe it has, then in my view it should provide the most clear example of the richest possession of self which is Christ-like and, following the example of the Master, is freely given to others through love. If this interpretation is correct, then its most urgent concern is to reverse its traditional preoccupation about the details of external appearances and work and concentrate on its internal life, which is primarily community life, as the basis of that development of self which will most accurately reflect the inner richness of Christ. No amount of external signs or work can remedy the defects of the inner life but, if this is close to Christ's own internal richness, then no external signs are required to demonstrate it. It is present in the expressions of love reflected in the quality of relationship to self and to others.

Now the mind of the Church clearly intends to help people achieve this sense of perfect love through the evangelical counsels of poverty, chastity and obedience and it is therefore pertinent to examine afresh these human characteristics in the light of modern understanding of the human personality. In case, which I hope is not the case, anyone is disturbed by what has been said so far, let me return to the document of Vatican II and quote one paragraph.

'Since the religious life is intended above all else to lead those who embrace it to an imitation of Christ and to union with God through the profession of the evangelical counsels, the fact must be honestly faced that even the most desirable changes made on behalf of contemporary needs will fail in their purpose unless a renewal of spirit gives life to them. Indeed such an interior renewal must always be accorded the leading role even in the promotion of exterior works.'

Article 2e of *Perfectae Caritas.*

As a psychiatrist what I understand by this is that the accent must be at all times on the ability to feel and to express love and that our way of life, while certainly doing justice to our intellect and social integrity, must at all times reflect love. Now love is the most potent word in the Christian – or indeed any other – vocabulary and the most difficult experience to realise. If Christ has lived on for two thousand years for those who do not believe in his divinity, he has done so by his unfaltering demonstration of love and the tragedy is that those who believe in his divinity do not always demonstrate this central characteristic. Thus, if the evangelical counsels have validity, this can only be within a framework of love in personal relationships. To interpret the advice given to the young man in the Gospel of St. Matthew of selling all his goods or the model of sexual continence in the passage above in isolation from personal relationships is a violation of the Christian message and, to the extent that religious life emphasised objectively the sacrificial elements of these vows without integrating them with the commandment of loving one's neighbour as oneself, it failed badly to realise its criterion of Christ-like behaviour. I would now like to examine the three evangelical counsels in the light of a contemporary understanding of personal relationships.

Chastity:

If we start with chastity, one brief definition of it has been the 'Deliberate renunciation of all voluntary use of one's power of generation'. Such a definition would indicate accurately the extreme poverty of the theology of this subject. Nor would fuller descriptions which emphasize the eschatological significance be all that helpful to those who have to live practically its implication.

In order to understand more fully the meaning of this virtue we must plunge into the depths of the human personality. Up to the time of Freud, human sexuality was seen in terms of post-pubertal sexual activity leading to intercourse with the powerful release of orgastic pleasure and possible fertilisation starting a new life. When people of the opposite sex met and acted in this way, such words as instinct, passion and love have been variously used to describe their behaviour. It has been the task of psychology to sharpen our awareness of the meaning of these words.

Freud first drew our attention to an infantile sexuality, or, put in another way, the characteristics we associate with sexuality and love in adult life have had their roots in a whole range of emotional behaviour which first took place in childhood. Thus the origins of love are to be found quite independently from adult sexual attraction and, indeed, the most important challenge in human relationships is how to fuse the emotions of love – whose foundations were laid in childhood – with adult sexual characteristics.

The characteristics which describe love are many and complex and take up millions of words in psychological texts. One feature stands out above others, namely that we are dealing with a world which is profoundly influenced by feelings and emotions.

In Western societies and traditional Christian education, much emphasis has been placed on the mind, intellect and will – the so-called rational, objective part of man which is contrasted with the subjective, emotional instinctual part. Frequently the former is designated in such terms as higher and the latter as lower. The symbol of the pyramid with the pinnacle standing for reason, equated with the masculine, and the base as the roots, reflecting the nurturing, the sustaining , the emotional and equated with the feminine is familiar to most people.

I hope that I will not be accused of pandering to a feminine audience if I say that much of this is the exaggerated fancy of a masculine dominated world which has been responsible for much injustice to women, is incompatible with a wealth of contemporary psychological knowledge, tends to fragment human beings and, above all, in a Christian setting, ignores the fact that the Son of Man experienced a wealth of emotions which allowed him to weep publicly, experience acute anxiety and demonstrate a tenderness and compassion which reflects a sensitivity and intuition that have remained shining examples for over two thousand years.

The combination of emphasis on the dangers of instinct and passion and the taboo on feelings of tenderness and affection and their expression has been a trend in all education, including Christian education. Thus dynamic psychology, which makes an exhaustive study of this area, was, and still is, seen as a dangerous threat to the, so-called, highest power of man's will which controls the lower elements.

Psychology has opened up the vista of human loving long before awareness of self or communication with others is carried on verbally or through logical operations. The major studies of the analytical psychologists and those of Piaget have given us massive new insights of the world of the first decade which remains a powerful infrastructure of human experience throughout life which does not have its primary source of experience in logic or thought but in the intimacy of physical and emotional contact and interaction. This aspect is often called irrational, disorderly, regarded with suspicion, feared and, up to now, has been most emphatically seen as a danger to be tightly controlled and suppressed.

In reality it is neither irrational nor disorderly nor dangerous. Once the parameters of human development are beginning to be comprehended, the various bits of the puzzle begin to fall into place and make sense. What is indisputable is that without this dimension man is impoverished and certainly cannot be considered Christ-like.

In those early years and in the pre-verbal phase of growth, the child learns the meaning of love through bodily communication of touch, looks, which are often that of smiling, and sound, which can be the gentle murmur of approval or the noisy cacophony of disapproval or desperation. All this exchange is a reciprocal one from the earliest possible moment, exhibiting the supremacy of mutuality and relationship in what we call love. The body remains the infrastructure throughout life of communicating love through touch, vision and sound.

As a result of this contact the sense of trust and security begins to emerge and remains of fundamental import thereafter. In the absence of trust, we cannot get close to people and they cannot get close to us. What happens in these circumstances is that we communicate through the intellect, social habit and custom without the inner world of feeling ever being reached. The outer self is reached, the inner self is untouched and this gap may be, and is often, unknown to all the participants who are under the illusion that they are really in touch with each other and with God. When this occurs in marriage, catastrophe may set in most unexpectedly by one or other partner finding a third party who can reach them and thus discovering for the first time after many years what love truly is.

In the presence of trust and security, the child gradually begins to feel recognized, wanted, valued, respected for its own separate existence and characteristics. Two dangers now exist. The first is that, instead of this positive growth or affirmation, the child experiences indifference or rejection. The second is that its separate and individual status is not recognized and it grows without any confidence in itself, a particular danger of authoritarian systems which can only treat the 'other' as an object whose 'goodness' only reflects the extent of blind, automatic obedience to authority.

Thus many, many people grow up shy, diffident, unable to register or feel their own significance, dependent on others for direction or purpose, outwardly very compliant and obedient but inwardly living in a world of emptiness and personal disapproval into which they have no insight.

Such a personality, showing the characteristics of sensitivity, without confidence, critical of itself, lacking in self-esteem, not infrequently in the past found refuge in a world of pseudo-humility, pseudo-obedience and pseudo-chastity.

Pseudo-humility reinforces the sense of self-abnegation in a person who has little, if any, sense of his own value. Pseudo-obedience is the outward manifestation of compliance and acceptance of authority because fear rules out the possibility of disagreement and immaturity dreads the assumption of initiative and personal responsibility. Pseudo-chastity is the expression of a failure of development of feelings, emotion or instincts to any sufficient degree so that the absence of demonstration of these elements in personal relationships relieves the person from responsibility for developing these vital elements of love.

The characteristics of love which the parent needs to show for the realisation of their child's potential is as follows. They are expected to be present in a relationship which shows continuity, reliability and predictability. Seventy-five years of psychological research is showing clearly the damage to the human personality when these characteristics are absent. In the presence of these characteristics, the parent acts as a source of sustenance, healing and growth for the child. The physical and intellectual growth are easy to demonstrate, the emotional most difficult but it is emotional healing and growth that remains the principal component in adult life. Physical sexuality is a powerful means of reinforcing the emotional sustenance, healing and growth of the spouses. This sustenance, healing and growth applies equally to the needs of all human beings and the ability to offer them to our neighbour is the principal expression of our love for them.

You may well ask what about meeting their material and intellectual needs? Certainly there is a need for this, but the gospels abound in the simple message that, beyond the material, the physical and the intellectual, lies the spiritual which means reflecting on God, having a relationship with him and, as a result of this, going on to feel and demonstrate this love to our neighbour and ourselves.

The breakthrough for contemporary Christianity must be the awareness that people are looking for love, healing and growth which go well beyond the traditional concepts of service to the body and mind. Certainly the sick and the poor remain with us and so do the children who need to be taught but all these, and particularly the children, will increasingly require another dimension which reflects the world of feeling, emotion and instinct. Now Christianity is particularly rich in this world and the real tragedy is that centuries of legalism have introduced an impersonalism and emotional aridity which has virtually atrophied the meaning of Christianity.

Thus, in this context, chastity can be described as emotional sincerity through which people grow in the understanding of the meaning of love now understood in terms of interpersonal trust, appreciation, development of potential, restoration of confidence, affirmation, open expression of feelings, the negotiation of conflict through forgiveness, reconciliation and reparation. The healing of past wounds, the enhancement of personal awareness, the growth in positive self-acceptance are essential ingredients of love in personal relationships and must form the central focus round which a religious community lives its life. It is through these relationships that each will have his or her self-esteem recharged so as to be able to empty themselves in giving these very same characteristics in the love they offer to others. The quality of this love undoubtedly reflects the internal experience of the person and can be briefly summarised thus:

I am capable of trusting others because I know the feeling of
trust and can trust myself:
I am capable of appreciating others because I know the feelings
of appreciation and can appreciate myself:

89

I am capable of investing others with significance because I
know the feeling of significance and I feel significant;
I am capable of feeling the good in others because I know the
feeling of goodness and feel good, at least sometimes.

Clearly such a conceptualisation of service to others transcends the
meeting of strictly social needs, be they educational, social, medical or
nursing. The emphasis now shifts to the quality of the relationship with
the person served, be they child or adult. Here above all, the meaning of
being a Christian will emerge, not only in identifying a need, which the
State or anybody else can do, but more in the quality of discharging
this need which must match the continuous total emptying of self in
the service of the other who is our neighbour. But the emptying must
not leave the person empty as our Lord clearly never was and likewise
the religious community must act as a constant source of recharging
each other.

This recharging is now done no longer through the exclusive
one-to-one relationship of marriage or the powerful reassurance of
sexual intercourse. In the absence of such powerful supports, clearly
the person entering religious life must either possess a high degree of
emotional integrity or the potential for its growth provided the
community can foster it and the council gives clear directions in this
matter.

'Since the observance of total continence intimately involves the
deeper inclinations of human nature, candidates should not under-
take the profession of chastity nor be admitted to its profession
except after a truly adequate testing period and only if they have the
needed degree of psychological and emotional maturity. They
should not only be warned of the dangers confronting chastity but
be trained to make a celibate life consecrated to God part of the
richness of their whole personality.'

Article 12 of *Perfectae Caritas*.

You may well ask what does this training consist of? In the last few
years much discussion has taken place about the nature of community
life. Its size, site, authority structure, and life of prayer have all stirred
much discussion which I have been privileged to share and contribute
to. Quite clearly there are no single answers. But there is one single
answer as far as the life of chastity is concerned.

If physical sexuality is a vital vehicle of communicating feelings of
recognition, acceptance, appreciation, in short love, then in its absence

there must be an increasing, open, rich, deep emotional encounter which can compensate for the loss of the physical. Vatican II here shows a deep insight simply expressed.

> 'Above all, everyone should remember — superiors especially — that chastity has stronger safeguards in a community when true fraternal love thrives amongst its members.'
>
> Article 12 of Perfectae Caritas.

I am convinced from varied and continuous contacts with religious that this is the only viable answer, and what is more, when the Christian motivation of love is coupled with the vast array of new insights brought together by the psychological sciences, then we have available to-day one of the most important breakthroughs for the extension of the kingdom of God in personal relationships.

Poverty

Is there a link between chastity just described and poverty? Most clearly so. Our Lord did not reject the rich who accepted the kingdom of God and, in an act of profound significance, accepted before his passion the anointing of his head with a very costly ointment. This is a beautiful illustration of the point I made earlier in that the emptying of Christ was a donation of his inner richness which was never lost and which could accept in the appropriate circumstance an external sign which matched this internal state.

The point about Christ's poverty is that he possessed himself so totally, so fully and richly that he did not need any external material possessions to support his internal world.

In my view it is vital to recognise that there is nothing intrinsically good in poverty as such and its relief is a necessary prerequisite for realising a minimum level of human dignity. Clearly the vow of obedience can never be used as a denial of this level of personal status. It is equally clear that no material wealth can establish a secure sense of self which can give the certainty that Christ possessed about his identity. Such certainty ultimately depended on a personal relationship of love and it is this inner certainty, based on relationships of love, needing no material or physical support, that the Christian life aims to achieve. If this interpretation is accepted, then clearly the material impoverishment becomes less and less of a burden as the inner certainty grows of who we are, where we come from and where we are heading for. For the Christian this is the kingdom of God which is based on love, love of God, neighbour and of self which is the foundation of our existence.

In a world desperately busy acquiring a developing sense of its dignity, in which material things play a prominent part, Christianity can

91

accept their intrinsic value and yet point the way beyond, now and eschatologically, when the only absolute reality is love in personal relationships. The religious community should be a leading example of the correct use of material goods for the proper dignity of its members but the quality of their relationship within and without should indicate even more clearly the next phase of personal realisation of wholeness – a wholeness which, as in the case of our Lord, was no longer embarrassed either by the necessity or the responsibility of material possessions.

Obedience:

What our Lord possessed completely and freely gave to others was himself, which leads to the final counsel of perfection and one which, it has to be admitted, is least understood at the present moment. This is inevitable in the midst of such a major transition in understanding the meaning of authority.

It is easier to say what obedience is not rather than what it is. The model must remain that of Christ and the obedience of Christ to His father is certainly not one of obedience by a lesser to a greater, by a child to an adult, by a subordinate to a superior, based on fear and inequality, backed by sanctions for disobedience.

This model so widespread in the Church until recently has absolutely nothing to do with Christianity and certainly nothing to do with Christ, whose obedience to the Father was that of voluntary acceptance, through love, of a task of redemption, shared by the Trinity in equality of status but with differentiating expressions.

The obedience of Christ to the Father was an obedience between equals and this implies that the intrinsic value, significance, status, meaning, in other words the wholeness of the second person, was in no way reduced by it. This has immense implications for the vow of obedience where similarly the intrinsic value, significance, status and meaning of the person must be most carefully safeguarded at all times. How is this to be safeguarded? There are of course no absolute answers but I am here quoting from a document called the *Bill of Rights* which appeared in the *Tablet* on 16th December, 1972 which, amongst many items, describes the responsibility of those in authority. It reads.

1. By virtue of the exercise of power some of the People of God will exercise authority over others.
2. None should allow himself to be placed in such a position without the consent, expressed or implied, of those over whom he will exercise authority.
3. In the exercise of authority, everyone is bound to conduct himself in accordance with the following principles:

(a) Those who exercise authority are the servants of those over whom they exercise it;

(b) Authority may only be exercised for the greater benefit and never to the detriment, of those who will be affected by its exercise;

(c) The exercise of authority serves the end of enlarging and not of restricting the rights of those who are affected thereby.

(d) Before authority can be exercised all persons likely to be substantially affected by its exercise must be given an adequate opportunity of being heard, and their views must be fairly taken into account;

(e) All authority must be exercised openly, unless express consent to the contrary is given by all those likely to be substantially affected;

(f) Except for the exercise of authority by the College of Bishops of the universal Church and its head, all exercise of authority must be subject to at least one appeal to a higher authority;

(g) All authority must be exercised in charity, humility, honesty and justice;

(h) All authority must be exercised in accordance with the law, save where mercy requires otherwise.

I am sure that, apart from arguable details, all would agree that, if authority behaves in this way, it eliminates some of the appalling scandals that have occurred in the past. It is true that the enemies of Christianity seize on these and make much of them but − and here I take an uncompromising stand − those whose life is meant to reflect most closely the relationship between Son and Father must ensure that their system of governing leaves few hostages to fortune.

Given that those in authority behave in this way and obedience safeguards at all times the dignity and value of the individual, what is its special virtue?

If we accept that obedience has nothing essentially to do with the relationship of one person in a structure of inequality and that is what I understand by Christ's obedience to the Father, then it becomes a freely given response of love in which the self is donated to others either as part of a common aim or as an individual commitment.

Seen in this context, obedience is most clearly related to the call of perfection. It is sometimes naively assumed that obedience is a virtue and responsibility specially assigned to those who take the vow. Of course nothing is further from the truth. Obedience in the sense discussed must be the daily experience of every Christian for whom every minute of day and night must remain open to the will of God.

In the narrow sense, obeying instructions from a superior, to the extent that one has freely given that person the right to act in this way, is of course something that everyone is subject to and has no special virtue. The virtue of obedience which truly reflects the Christian message is ultimately offering the availability of oneself, out of love for the sake of another.

Thus I see the evangelical counsels in an ascending order of perfection creating a sense of wholeness in the person, springing from a growing sense of identity which the virtue of chastity gives, reaffirmed by the vow of poverty which shows that the possession of self is an ever growing emotional experience, independent of material support, leading ultimately to the total availability of self to conform totally to the will of God and be equally totally available to love neighbour and self. By love of self is, of course, meant increasing awareness and possession of every part of oneself which is positively accepted and therefore available to others in two ways. The first is that the more of oneself one recognizes the more of others is recognized too and secondly less of others has to be rejected because there is less of self which is threatened by them.

Thus I see obedience as being related to availability which is the *raison d'être* of the single person and an availability now centred on an increasingly inner recognition and acceptance of self which then becomes readily available to others.

Community

Such a vision of the single person places vital importance on the community which must be the place where the sustaining, healing, growth and recharging of the individual takes place. The order of priority thus becomes availability to each other for this growth in perfection in community, from which springs availability to others through work. Work, of course, has its own justification in reinforcing the identity of the person but in the religious life it becomes a powerful instrument of availability of service to others. The point I am trying to make is that, although of course there must be a delicate balance between the life of the community and the work it carries out, the priority lies in the former.

It may be objected that this makes the community an inward looking, selfish, self centred place. My own feeling in this matter is unequivocal. What the world needs most urgently at the present moment is a variety of models of human community which can show how members can treat each other with respect, accord human dignity, have regard for individual freedom and foster the realisation of their potential while living in an atmosphere of peace, trust and — above all — love. Christianity has two such basic models, the home and the religious community in its various forms and I sincerely believe that, far from reaching a historic moment of their conclusion, they are at the dawn of another breakthrough where members will be of little significance in themselves but the Christ-like quality of living together will be of paramount importance in a world that has deliberately turned its back on the institutional Church, whose formal voice and pre-occupation appear too distant, and is eagerly looking for Christ in the immediacy of living.

EMOTIONAL MATURITY AND THE PRIESTHOOD

Introduction

The advent of Vatican II has introduced a whole series of innovations which are being slowly incorporated into the life of the people of God. Many of them are expressed directly in the form of changes in worship and liturgy; others in matters of structure and organisation. All of them are and still remain ideological controversies. Some topics, such as those affecting the nature of authority, have produced continuous, at times acrimonious, difficulties. In order to polarize discussion, labels have been given: "conservative" to denote an attachment to the traditions of the past, and "progressive" to the orientation and desire for change, slow or rapid. These terms have their use but in no way adequately describe the complex issues involved. There are too many Catholics who hold "conservative" views in one area and "progressive" ones in another and vice versa. The norm is an admixture which reflects often the sociological and psychological make-up of the individual.

The behavioural sciences of sociology, psychology, anthropology, etc., have been examining the phenomenon of man for over a hundred years but most intensively in this century and particularly during the last fifty years. Unfortunately, like so much else of the contemporary scene, they were regarded with suspicion, uncertainty and mistrust when compared with the certainty of the philosophical and theological approach taught in the seminaries and permeating the life of the Church. One major factor responsible for Vatican II, and in fact for renewal, was the massive and ever growing gap between the view of man seen in these traditional terms imbued with a closed, legalistic, static thinking and the contemporary, open, non-judgemental, dynamic view of man. Here the sciences of sociology and psychology have provided us with vital information for a penetrating understanding of the nature of man and a framework of reference which includes an extensive new language. This language is new to many, and communication between the various disciplines remains one of the urgent tasks of the present phase.

But granted that communication can be established, there are still nagging and worrying questions; namely, to what extent can these sciences ever be an adequate substitute for a Christian way of life? The answer is, of course, they are not meant to be. But neither was the legalistic framework in which generations of Catholics grew up.

96

Christian life has to pay detailed attention to human nature as it is lived and experienced afresh each age. At no other period has so much new information been brought to our attention. Not everything that is new will stand the test of time, but to ignore the authentic part is ultimately a rejection of the deepening awareness of the image of God unfolding in man. But the objective facts which can be welcomed have to be lived within the continuous transformation of all life brought about by the Incarnation. Hence psychological and sociological data are essential to do justice to our humanity, but for the Christian their ultimate meaning can only be understood within the living tradition of the Good News. There is no future in trying to isolate Christianity from man's deepening consciousness of himself, nor is it possible to do full justice to these new discoveries without illuminating them with the light of faith. The behavioural scientist who is also a Christian remains aware of the two layers of experience and ignores either at the risk of violating part or even the whole of the truth.

Personality, Role and Identity

The word personality, which is frequently used to describe diverse aspects of human behaviour, is derived from the Latin *persona* which originally meant a mask. In the theatrical world and on other occasions masks are used both to hide the real person and to convey some emotional feature such as fear, joy, laughter, etc. In contemporary terms, personality has been separated into two technical terms; namely *role* and *identity*. Role is the term used by sociologists and refers to the functioning and behaviour shaped by social expectations at home, work and in the community at large.

Thus the traditional roles of the husband implied that he was expected to function as head of the family with the duties and responsibilities of earning the income, directing the main goals of activity, negotiating the family's needs externally with the community and having ultimate authority. The wife, on the other hand, was mainly concerned with the care of the home internally, looking after the children, providing the affective atmosphere of warmth and tenderness, all in a subordinate status to her husband. These centuries-old traditions and roles are subjects of extensive changes currently and are influencing a major Christian preoccupation: namely family life.

Outside the home the relationship between employer and employee is also changing dramatically and the role expectations of both are altering to fit a social structure based less and less on authority and fear and more on a new balance of power based on supply and demand, with powerful trade union organizations safeguarding the interests of the workers. Education in general has also been transformed, so that the roles of teacher and pupil are no longer considered in terms of

97

active imparting of information to passive reception and acquisition. On the contrary, the relationship is now seen as a mutual involvement in which both parties are influenced by each other and the accent is on growth through activity, physical and mental: development through self-actualization and the greater possible realization of potential. Whatever aspect of life is examined, an evolution is to be seen in which all or some of the following points may be observed. The fixed, static pre-ordained relationship based on authority conferred by virtue of office, society or tradition no longer automatically carries absolute deference. Increasingly, authority and power are shared in an inter-dependent manner and, even more important, the characteristics of the individual or the organization rather than the tacit assumption of a particular office become the credentials for a comprehensive response. This is seen particularly in the ability of traditional sources of authority, for example teachers, doctors, lawyers and the police, to command respect from those they serve. The emphasis is on service rather than automatic obedience and the priest is very much part and parcel of this social revolution, bringing him, of course, very much closer to the spirit of Christ and the gospels.

Behaviour based on a sense of duty, responsibility, precise rewards for co-operation and exacting penalties for violation of the rules, aided by a sense of awe, fear, shame and guilt, which played such a prominent part in maintaining the social framework, is being challenged by the sense of commitment to reality, adherence through personal and considered choice, avoidance of hypocrisy, a stripping of outer signs and symbols to reveal the inner person, no longer buttressed by ceremonial dress or forms of address. Symbols which clarified social relationships, in a matter of seconds have been altered beyond recognition. The Church − which was deeply involved in this social system − is in the throes of the tensions arising from these modifications.

These social changes make heavy demands on the personality of the individuals who can no longer pursue the familiar. Here the world of roles which determines social group-defined activity meets the deeper layer of the person described by the psychological sciences with the word identity.

The word identity is not a precise one, but in general it describes the evolving consciousness of a self which carried both the enduring and changing characteristics of a person in different phases of life. The psychological factors which contribute to the identity are many, but include the person's endowments in terms of intelligence, perception, cognition, conation, integration and adaption; affectivity, in terms of anxiety, mood and capacity to experience and communicate feelings: and global patterns of behaviour such as extroversion, introversion, neuroticism and many other categories.

A great deal of the discussion arising from the changes brought about by Vatican II considers largely the social role implications of the theological and liturgical changes arising from the council. There is, however, a critical personal meeting point between the sociological and the psychological. Changes of *role* meet at some point the *identity* resources of the individual. If the *identity* cannot support the *role* changes or the role changes bring about completely different psychological expectations, there develops a profound conflict within the individual which expresses itself either slowly or suddenly and is usually accompanied by much unhappiness and anxiety expressed in different ways. The experience of the author suggests that the reasons for the departure of many priests and nuns from the religious life have little to do with the formal presence of psychiatric illness, but rather with the arrival of the individual at a critical socio-psychological meeting point which demands a radical change in life style. The sooner this truth is grasped by the Church, the sooner detailed attention can be given to remedy the situation which is going by default at present, on the false assumption of the presence of psychiatric illness or ascribing to individuals a poor sense of duty, or even a betrayal of Christ. The rest of this article will consider a few such crucial meeting points and evaluate them in terms of the word maturity.

Maturity

Before doing so, something needs to be said about the word maturity which is another term widely used but not easily capable of precise definition. Maturity in the biological sense of adult height, weight, length and size of various organs, or their functions such as the pre- and post-pubertal activity of the sexual organs is capable of reasonably clear measurement. Intelligence, which is in itself a complex phenomenon, is also capable of measurement. Other traits, such as anxiety and mood levels, can also be assessed but here measurement becomes much less precise and continues to become less so when we describe other aspects of personality. Many would agree that maturity includes the ability to anticipate danger, to take the necessary steps for self-preservation and to control the instincts of sexuality and aggression. A reasonable measure of judgement, initiative, patience and capacity to negotiate frustration, the ability to tolerate aloneness, failure and rejection and the positive ability to register and express feelings, particularly those concerned with affection, tenderness and love also belong to it. Over and above the control of excessive aggression, maturity implies the negotiation of conflict, the ability to forgive and to accept forgiveness and the avoidance of revenge. The list can grow to any length depending on individual choice but there are certain contemporary factors which emphasize special aspects of maturity.

For example, following Freudian and dynamic psychology in general a great deal of emphasis has been laid on feelings, emotions and instincts, characteristics which did not hold prominence until recent times. The traditional emphasis on reason and the intellect is being complemented by an existential emphasis on the capacity to experience and express feelings adequately. The balance between suppression and expression is a delicate matter subject to continuous current discussion. With the emphasis shifting towards greater expression and coupled with a reduction of ritual and respect for authority we have a familiar and controversial debate as to what really constitutes mature behaviour.

Another feature of contemporary life is the massive orientation towards independence and the greatest possible realization of freedom and self-determination. These features contrast with the recent emphasis on dependence, graduated and controlled assumption of responsibility, constant reference to authority and strict adherence to the rules. Instead of rigid and blind appliance of a legalistic framework, every encouragement is being given to self-actualization through personal exploration, self-verification and relentless examination of whatever is being taken for granted.

Many will argue that these and similar changes, far from being steps towards maturity, are the mounting edifices of chaos, disorder and the gradual dissolution of a stable framework of society and, inside the Church, of faith. Anything carried to excess has its dangers, of course, and independence, freedom and challenge of the law, pursued relentlessly for their own sake independently of the needs of society as a whole or the good of the individual, are potentially damaging. It is a matter of judgement, however, whether these dangers are greater than those which were present before; namely excessive security without openness or growth, dependence which ultimately stifled initiative and infantilized the individual, and blind obedience to law which dehumanized by denying so much of man's inner world. The tension between the external and the internal present in the Scriptures is seen anew today in man with the psychological sciences emphasizing the inner world in terms of conscious and unconscious forces, shaped and dominated by feelings and emotional needs whose origins are to be found in childhood and whose development reflects an important aspect of maturity.

The advantages and disadvantages of the new and the old will continue to provide the material for debate and controversy, but the issues under discussion are of paramount importance when considering the maturity of the contemporary priest. Some of these elements which repeat themselves in common patterns and situations can now be examined.

Dependence – Independence

The emphasis placed by society on self-determination is closely related to a major factor of natural development. One aspect of the human personality can be comprehensively described in the movement of all human beings from total dependence on their parents in the early years to the gradual acquisition of independence, so that by the end of the second decade the young person is ready to accomplish three vital events. These are the detachment from home, the negotiation of independent work and the establishment of heterosexual relationships ultimately leading to courtship and marriage.

Each of these processes is a complex phenomenon whose achievement is determined by the personal predisposition of the individuals, the type of upbringing they have received and the prevailing mores in society regarding the assumption of personal responsibility. Considering these three elements in reverse, young people are as free in their adolescence and as responsible as society determines appropriate. At this moment we are living through a period in which the accent is on the greatest possible freedom and the earliest possible assumption of personal responsibility. The characteristics of the recent past in which young people were closely supervised, overprotected and denied self-determination at this stage of their development are being superseded. As far as the priesthood is concerned, such a movement has clear implications for junior seminaries, which are no longer seen as providing the appropriate setting for the maturation of a future priest. Instead of focusing on a narrow range of experience, it is now considered important that young men and women should be encouraged to handle the emotional issues related to separation from home with its attendant loneliness, to tackle the problems of work and to learn something of their sexual identity in personal relationships.

A considerable number of priests and nuns have left their vocation precisely on these grounds, and the Church has paid a heavy price for a mistaken interpretation that an early vocation denoted singular dedication. In individual instances this was true, but as a whole entry at a very young age meant that the emotional dependence of adolescence was maintained in a structure and organization within the Church which perpetuated this dependence and was inimical to personal growth. Thus many priests and nuns continued to grow in their twenties and thirties and, as soon as the atmosphere within the Church made it possible, left in relatively large numbers. It can be safely stated that the single most important reason for this exodus is late maturation in which the appropriate goals of adolescence are reached in the late twenties, thirties and sometimes in the forties and even fifties.

This is a phenomenon of maturation of the personality and has absolutely nothing to do with psychiatric illness. Furthermore, when such men and women have spent many years in their vocation, the urgent need to leave and experience their life in totally different ways clashes violently with their deep-rooted habits and loyalties. The conflict is often deep and painful and is not made any easier when their own inner perplexity is interpreted in a hostile or critical way. In psychological terms their situation can be understood readily and comprehensively. They themselves only feel the need for freedom, personal responsibility and the need to experience their identity as sexual beings in a deeper sense. These features can be interpreted as flouting authority, irresponsibility and a betrayal of chastity. When one considers for a moment their previous dedication it is hardly likely that they would change so completely as to devalue all that was precious to them before. Instead, the answer is often to be found in their growing realization that their present situation is inimical and irrelevant to their life. Until recently this discovery would not have met with any public recognition or approbation and so their departure would have been furtive and secret, if at all. Now it is an open event but its very openness is in fact rightly preparing the Church to recognize the psychological fact that those entering the single state, dedicated to God, should have already negotiated the essential steps of adolescence.

This recognition in a sociological sense alone will not be enough. Even if junior seminaries and early entry to the priesthood are discouraged, there will still be individuals who, as a result of various types of upbringing and their own personal idiosyncrasies, may still be drawn by the apparent structural security of the priesthood. Without realizing it, they may still be seeking an alternative to the engagement of secular life which is too anxiety-provoking for them. Thus continuous care and vigilance should be exercised in assessing all individuals despite the presence and appearance of all the appropriate attributes of a vocation.

In fact, the training for the priesthood should test any such underlying immaturity by including a programme which allows for the development of openness, undeterred questioning, the assumption of personal responsibility, experimentation, awareness and participation with a whole variety of living conditions in society and the feeling of involvement with the people of God for whose service they are preparing themselves. Such a training will mean that, if they question and challenge their teachers now, this is only a preparation for a situation where they in turn will be quesioned, challenged and probed by a world that is desperately seeking God and is extremely sceptical of all organized religion. This prevailing attitude of the second half of the twentieth century has to be recaptured deliberately within the training period. Just as Christ prepared himself for the doubts, cynicism, criticism and hostility of the society to which he sought to reveal himself, so the priest of tomorrow, imitating the Lord, has to prepare himself to face the groups of men and women seeking the love of God in personal terms quite different from those of even a decade ago.

Openness – Closeness

The word openness has appeared several times in this article and will now be considered in some detail. Openness and closeness are intimately associated with the presence or absence of an authoritarian system of social functioning. Within such a system everyone has a recognised position with circumscribed limits of responsibility and involvement with those above and below. When publicly agreed limits are reached, there is no further possibility of communication. Furthermore, these limits are themselves an expression of sanctioned traditions largely regulated by a legal framework of reference.

This is not to say that society or the Church can function without order or law. The Catholic Church has been admired, and rightly so, for its clarity, precision and systematic approach to its spiritual life and organization. But these very virtues have become an embarrassment, as excessive reliance on law is ultimately a restriction or strangulation of growth, development and the essential renewal of life. The primary challenge facing the Catholic Church is finding a way of life that retains the virtues of a stable and continuous framework of reference without violating the rapid evolution in man's growing consciousness of himself. The tension within the Church over every major development betrays this conflict and provokes controversy between those who wish to protect the Church from jettisoning the familiar advantages of rules and regulations and those who insist that man's spirit must, as in the Scriptures, have the primacy of attention at all times.

This post-Vatican II challenge faces every person in the Church, and particularly the priest who has to assist the people he serves to reach the appropriate balance in their own lives. But in order to do this for others he must have attained some perspective in this matter within himself. Endless correspondence in Catholic papers, journals, and speeches at public meetings, shows the various positions which are reached. As stated before, the words "conservative" and "progressive" are too global to do justice to such a complex matter. There are of course, people holding extreme positions in either direction, but the majority find themselves considering each individual matter on its own merits. Papal authority, collegiality, birth control, marriage of the clergy, co-responsibility, Catholic schools, mixed marriages, liturgical changes, ecumenism, etc., all elicit a whole variety of attitudes. Behind such diversity are there any common psychological attributes which can assist in understanding personal positions? It is dangerous to over-simplify in psychological matters as in anything else. And yet closeness and openness ultimately depend on the personal confidence and security of the individual and ultimately of the community concerned. According to one's security in one's own identity, and in one's faith in Christ as Lord, Saviour and second person of the Trinity, so an openness to change can be tolerated. It is faith in oneself and in Christ and not simply in law which matters. If faith is built merely on adherence to the letter of the law, then every change from the familiar and the habitual is a threat to security and is experienced as a signal with dire consequences to be resisted defensively.

To the extent that the Church relied heavily on the security of a legal framework, it also appealed to men and women whose own personality required the maximum security which they found in the corresponding structures within it. Every change for such a person is potentially dangerous, not because it is evaluated with Christ's message as the external criterion of truth, but simply because change generates anxiety and is a threat to personal security. In psychological terms, the significance of Vatican II lies in the way the Spirit has taken hold of the hand of the people of God, the Church, and is guiding them to new insights without the fear or panic of being overwhelmed by the new and the unknown.

The collective openness of the people of God has to be matched by that of the individual priest, and here personal characteristics are of great importance. There is need not only for openness to all that is taking place collectively inside the Church but equally for an openness to oneself. As behaviour is shaped and controlled less and less in a standardized, impersonal and legalistic way from the centre, the individual is left a great deal more scope to cope with his own personal resources. Such a decentralization and assumption of personal respon-sibility has been welcomed by many but for some it is an intolerable burden which generates a great deal of anxiety. There is a small group of priests and nuns who have left their vocation for this reason, which is exactly the opposite of that responsible for the majority of departures. The absence of the recognized symbols of order and organization has deprived such individuals of much, if not all, of the meaning of the priesthood and the resultant vacuum has proved overwhelming. Many others have experienced this same impoverishment with the passing of the familiar but their faith has persisted even if the new symbols are temporarily blurred and confusing.

The future will demand a new way of life for the priest in which flexibility, innovation and adaptability will be crucial characteristics. With the rapidity of evolution facing advanced industrial societies, the Church will have to equip itself with structures that can respond with equal speed, sensitivity and imagination and the priest will have to be at the forefront of this Church constantly open to the Spirit. *Stability will lie less in unchangeable structures and far more in fidelity to the unchanging principles of the faith which will be communicated in new ways.*

Such a way of life demands from the priest an openness to himself as a person and this experience is fundamentally entirely psychological in nature, psychological in the sense that personal security and its attendant flexibility, acceptance of oneself as a person worthy to give and to receive love, awareness of one's own feelings, the ability to communicate these feelings and to empathize with the emotional needs of others will provide the foundation of pastoral life in the future. The priest who recognizes all this in himself will also recognize it in his encounter with men and women also seeking these deeper layers of personal significance in their own lives and in their relationships.

Deepening personal sensitivity results from close and effective communication with others. Registering and reflecting on these encounters can disclose unconscious aspects about ourselves not open to our own reflexions. This demands a much greater emphasis on community living and interaction and much less on impersonal, isolated, detached activity. Here the Church has its own internal resources of wisdom in the life of religious which it can share with the secular clergy but all groups have to learn new levels of interaction in personal contact which were considered strange and dangerous up to recently. The priest visited his parishioners but responded at a distance. There were many barriers to be pulled down both by him and his people in order to reach an intimate level of personal interaction. But it is this very intimacy which characterized Christ's relationship with his apostles and those who came close to him, and this characteristic has to be lived afresh in our day and time. This intimacy is, of course, present in the new liturgy with the priest facing the people at mass, the use of the vernacular, the mutual involvement in running the parish, etc. But of course in practice it has to go much further than this minimum. One of the vital sacraments is that of marriage and, in this above all, the priest of the future has to make personal and intimate contact with married couples, understanding and encouraging their own personal growth and helping them with their development as a family. Here the Church is faced with one of the major revolutionary changes, which has hardly begun, to arrange pastoral activity to meet the changing needs of several phases in the marriage cycle, the priest having to accompany and become a vital person in the life of the Christian family. He will have to be involved with the married as individuals, as a marital dyad, as parents and with their children and be able to respond with sensitivity to marriage, now experienced increasingly in terms of a relationship. This will be an encounter in which feelings will be of the greatest importance and whose success will depend on the most intimate involvement with the hopes, aspirations, fears, disappointments, failures and successes of the married who are now entering into an entirely new way of realizing their state.

Marriage and Sexuality

It may well be asked how is the priest to achieve such personal sensitivity in the absence of marriage? There are those who would maintain that it cannot be done and the sooner the Church abandons its stand on celibacy the better. The present author feels that such an attitude would lead to an impoverishment of the Christian community and a loss of one of the most precious contributions of the Catholic Church.

If however, the characteristics described in this article, which can be summed up as sensitivity, intimacy, openness, flexibility, self-determination, self-reliance and an emphasis on love rather than law, become universally accepted as the mature features of the priesthood for the future, then clearly the choice, training and personal experience of the priest will have to alter.

First of all it should be said at once that marriage in no sense guarantees the development of these features which can be possessed by the single just as much as the married. Contemporary marriage, however, experienced much less as a contract of duties and obligations and much more as an intimate relationship, demands a personal closeness between the spouses themselves and their children which encourages the nurturing of these characteristics. Such deepening of communication at an emotional level is not without its risks and many casualties of marriage are precisely failures to achieve a minimum emotional stability. But for the majority the daily intimate encounter, with sexual intercourse acting as a powerful instinctual and emotional force, activates mutual needs which bring a response from the emotional depths of the individual.

What can take the place of marriage for the priest? Without the instinctual and emotional development within marriage, it is clear that the personality of the individual must carry these characteristics in a nascent or developed sense at the time of entry. Thus the features of the personality which will be desirable will be precisely those which allow the person to have access to his emotions and instincts and accept both without anxiety or the need to deny them. In no sense can the priest of tomorrow, who will have to function in a society profoundly conscious of the significance of sexuality, succeed unless he feels and accepts sufficiently his own sexuality without conscious or unconscious rejection, envy or alienation of others who live it fully in their marriage.

Only by communicating to others approval and acceptance of sexuality can priests transcend the gap between their own sexual experience and those of others, thus becoming available to others struggling to find themselves through it. Like Christ, who could respond fully to others because he encountered in them nothing which he did not find and accept within himself, so the priest who will be communicating with his people at this deeper level must be able to do so with a realistic and positive sense of self-acceptance.

But if the sexual intimacy of marriage is not available to challenge and deepen self-awareness then clearly the life of the priest, both in training and later on, must have adequate substitutes in other words, strong emotional bonds with people of both sexes. This is easier to advocate than to arrange but within the love and security generated by Christian principles it should be possible to maintain close ties with people of one's own sex and with proper safeguards with the opposite sex, so that the necessary emotional encounter for personal growth can be found.

The Church is still concerned with the risks that such intimate community life will involve. The answer clearly is that, if a man is not ready or capable of having close emotional relationships with people of his own sex and the opposite without being sexually involved, then he is not really pursuing the right vocation and the sooner this is discovered the better.

The exact arrangements will vary from one situation to another and some are already taking place in mixed training programmes at universities and elsewhere. But closeness and interaction must not stop at the training period. It will continue in parish life where the priest has to be one with his people and be able to feel and to respond to their needs and yet, at the same time, pursue his own internal growth vertically with God.

Such qualities are of course rare and the accent on vocation must always be on quality and not numbers: nor does such a view preclude the possibility that both single and married clergy may be needed. And yet, if the people of God can agree on the type of Christian community they wish to foster, there is no reason to fear that men and women will choose freely any less now than in the past to make themselves fully available for the sake of the Kingdom.

Universality

But such availability must be truly catholic. In a period of such variability and transition the needs of the community will be equally variable. It will be a mistake to assume that the characteristics described in this article will be the only ones needed by a Church that has to serve many communities at different stages of development. The materially deprived in the under-developed world are still with us and will be so for a very long period. But this mixture only emphasizes the need for flexibility and a system which does not mistake rigidity for catholicity. The fact is that whatever the pace, all societies are moving in the direction of the advanced communities of the West and, if Christianity is going to be relevant, then it must convey its eternal message in ways that will be seen and recognized, heard and understood. Beyond the social and psychological changes must be experienced the eternal truths of the Kingdom of God in whose fields the labourers of tomorrow have to be no less mature, although in a different way to those of yesterday.

PART III

The two essays in this section were first given at Spode House to superiors of religious orders. Their basic theme is our encounter with God on the basis of our psychological development. In the light of this development prayer is seen as the language of our encounter with the 'Significant Other'.

PSYCHOLOGY OF PRAYER I

Introduction

The title of these two essays, namely the psychology of prayer, introduces both my general and specific approach to the subject and the way I am trying to tackle it in a whole range of issues.

The general approach refers to my central conviction that we cannot do any justice to our spiritual experience unless we understand as much as we can about the nature of our humanity. Since religion is an experience that involves the mysterious, much of its description has necessarily a language which sounds appropriately spiritual like soul, spirit, grace, etc. All these words have received immense attention over the centuries but we can never do justice to their reality if we ignore, confuse, and misunderstand the depths of our humanity. Now I believe that this is precisely what has happened in the last hundred years. We have fallen into the most dangerous trap of believing that, if we concentrate sufficiently on the sacred, the secular or the profane will look after itself. Christianity is paying an extremely heavy price for this error.

All of us grew up with the religious teaching that, if we prayed, attended Church, received the sacraments and obeyed the teaching of the Church, all would be well. Despite the apparent sense in this approach, we find ourselves in a world in which the majority treat all these instructions as irrelevant and yet long to find God and those, the small minority, who still follow these principles, find themselves divided and confused. This confusion leads to petty squabbling between the faction who believe that all will be well if only we do what the Church has instructed us to do and others who are convinced that, while holding on to the essentials of the Christian tradition, nothing else but a radical reexamination of our practices will lead to a renewal of religious experience. I belong firmly in this latter group and bring to this examination the conviction that the immediate future of religion requires an enormous updating of the psychological understanding of our humanity without which we are trying to respond to God with an image of man that no longer corresponds to our understanding of ourselves.

The specific approach concerns the subject of prayer which is the theme of this conference. One very ancient and honoured definition of

110

prayer is 'speaking to God', and the psychological examination will begin with this.

The Concept of Relationship and Prayer:

The immediate aftermath of this brief description of prayer is to ask the questions – what is the nature of the speaker, what the nature of God, and what is the link between them? The speaker is us, men and women, a tangible, recognisable reality and the first point to make about us is that our nature is steeped in relationships. All human beings begin their existence in a state of relationship, no less than nine months in the womb of their mother. Until man decides to bypass the human womb, which is one of the moral challenges slowly gathering momentum, all life begins in a relationship with another human being and continues throughout life in a variety of intimate and more distant relationships. Relationship is of the essence of being human and the spiritual is defined by the moment to moment relationship between man and God, of which prayer is one vital form of communication.

The Nature of Relationship:

In order to understand this moment to moment relationship between man and God, we have to plunge into the depths of human nature to clarify as clearly as possible the nature of our human experiences which are the only means of relating to God. I have purposely written 'the only means' in order to avoid the perpetual confusion which surrounds this topic when we touch on matters of mysticism, visions and the extraordinary in man's experience of God. These are subjects of utter fascination and far too little understood, although what understanding there is is largely related to psychological parameters. Be that as it may, what I want to emphasize here is that, even when we are near to these experiences, man's nature is not suspended. What is occurring is a particular mode of behaviour which allows physical and psychological perception of an unusual order but, unless the miraculous is occurring in unequivocal terms, everything has an explanation which is strictly within the confines of human potentiality. All these modes of experiencing God are no more or less truly spiritual for those who have them than for those who do not. I do not believe God is bestowing any special privileges on those whose personality allows them to feel in this way and certainly Christian spirituality would benefit enormously if it stopped being lured by these rare phenomena as if they were precious prizes or accolades for spiritual athletes. Our spirituality, which always reflects the quality of our individual relationship with God, does not depend on the mode of experience. What does it depend on? If we trace human development, we can see the outline of the answer which lies in understanding man's consciousness of himself, firstly in his individual,

111

personal growth and secondly in the cultural climate of his community and age which influences his own understanding of himself.

Personal development – Physical awareness:

The roots of our personality undoubtedly lie in the physical, a notion which bedevils Christianity in particular and all religions, because the sense of God par excellence does not lie in the immediacy of physical recognition and social contact, hence the constant problem of differentiating between what belongs to God genuinely and what image of God is fashioned by man which is a projection of our earthly understanding. The problem of idolatry, anthropomorphic divinities, the sacrilegious, the celebration of the orgiastic, all indicate man's difficulty in distinguishing between the physical transformed by imagination and the divine which is uncreated and totally self contained. Christianity finds the answer in the incarnation, in Christ, hence the paramount importance of a renewal of study and concentration on the Scriptures which focus and bring us near to this vital bridge between us and God.

Nevertheless each one of us has a personality which owes a substantial part to the physical. Christianity, while fighting the heresies which make of the carnal something evil, has an enormous amount of leeway to make up in order to return to the central significance of the physical, which existed in the Old Testament and in the New, and this in particular relationship to human sexuality, which is so central to the fullness of being human.

All of us begin life in a relationship which is totally physical in nature and we learn to communicate most profoundly with our bodies before speech develops. One cannot exaggerate the significance of this exchange.

If we return for a moment to the brief definition of prayer, namely speaking to God, we might make the false interpretation of this in confining prayer strictly to the process of speech or the surrounding psychological processes of thought, logical order of thought and verbal expression of it. If we do, we are, of course, making a fundamental error which alas Western civilisation is only too prone to do by attaching far too much significance to the intellectual processes of man which are connected with the mind, thought, logic and its verbal or written articulation. Speaking implies communication and that brief definition of prayer would in my view be greatly improved if the word communication is substituted for speaking, because the baby is already communicating with mother without words in the first year of life. The baby is communicating with mother by its awareness of her presence. Awareness of another person is at the heart of relationship and at the heart of prayer which is concerned with the sense of the presence of God.

The child's awareness of mother in the first three years of life is principally through physical contact. The two make contact through physical touch, visual exchanges such as smiles, frowns, expressions of confusion, anxiety, anger, puzzlement, all of which give the feeling of closeness and distance, approval or disapproval, feelings which are also communicated by sound. The words of mother are not understood by the child and the babbling of the child is equally incomprehensible to mother until about the second year when words are being formed. The absence of words does not diminish the intimacy of the exchange and this non-verbal intimacy remains with us throughout life.

This non-verbal intimate awareness of another person is vital for the understanding of prayer.

Non-Physical Communication:

Some of you feel perfectly at home with the notion of silent prayer, it is after all a familiar practice in our lives. Private meditation, contemplation which can alternatively be called mental prayer, speaking to God without making sounds, and that ghost from the past, silent retreats, are all perfectly familiar notions. But what appears perfectly ordinary and familiar is nothing of the kind because, if we eliminate all the physical signs of communication, that is to say physical touch, vision and sound, we have the task of retaining the sense of awareness of the missing person.

As far as the young child is concerned, out of sight, also means loss of awareness of another person, hence the enormous anxiety which it experiences in the first three or four years of life when it is physically separated from its mother. At this stage out of sight means literally lost for all eternity because each second of absence can become an eternity, a feeling of total loss. It is only in the third and fourth year that mother can begin to exist inside the child as a psychological reality in the absence of her physical presence. This psychological reality exists and deepens with the passing of years but remains a central psychological issue in all human relationships. How much continuing awareness of another person can we have in their physical absence or, even more important, how much of the other person can we experience and are therefore able to receive inside us in their actual presence?

There can be no doubt that this is a central psychological issue for prayer. What is our sense of God, our personal awareness, our image, our experience of the divine mystery in the absence of any physical experience of Him? You will remember the touching incident in the gospels which immortalised the significance of this for all time. Jesus had appeared to the apostles in the absence of Thomas.

'Thomas called the Twin, who was one of the Twelve, was not with them when Jesus came. When the disciples said — "We have seen the Lord," he answered, "Unless I see the holes that the nails made in his hands and can put my finger into the holes they made, and unless I can put my hand into his side I refuse to believe." Eight days later the disciples were in the house again and Thomas was with them. The doors were closed but Jesus came in and stood among them. "Peace be with you," he said. Then he spoke to Thomas: "Put your finger here; look, here are my hands. Give me your hand, put it into my side. Doubt no longer but believe." Thomas replied, "My Lord and my God." '

Jesus said to him:

"You believe because you can see me,

Happy are those who have not seen and yet believe." '

John 20: 24-29

Christ recognized the nature of the conflict and gave an answer which will stand until the end of time. It is also an answer which is relevant to the growth of all human beings in their individual development. As the years pass, the intensity of communication becomes less physical and extends in two directions, namely the world of feelings and that of intellectual development. Since feelings are of infinitely greater importance, these will be tackled first.

Affective Communication:

One of the grave weaknesses in Western thought is the enormous emphasis it has placed on the dichotomy between the physical and instinctual, and the associated body-mind duality. Feelings and emotions seem to exist so often in the idealised world of literature, drama and music where they are recognised and respected as such but treated as if they were not so easily related to the body-mind dichotomy. If my reading of this situation is remotely correct, then it exposes a fundamental crisis in Western thought and Christianity as experienced in the West, namely that human experience recognizes the world of feelings but has not integrated them in every day experience in the same way that the impact of the physical and intellectual has been registered and considered. I believe that this is one of the epoch making moments in the history of Western society and the psychological sciences, part of which are concerned primarily with feelings and instincts. These sciences have a unique contribution to make to the reconciliation of Western Christian thought with the essence of its message, which is love.

Now how is love mediated between child and parent in the next phase after the intensely physical encounter of the first five years? Technically this can be referred to as affective communication. Affect is a word with several meanings, one of which is exclusively concerned

114

with the dimension of feelings and emotions.

There are certain psychological features of the affective communication which are not subject to controversy. Through the physical we receive recognition. We shake hands, we smile, we greet each other with words. This establishes a minimum level of communication and the acts of private and public prayer, worship and liturgy are the means of establishing the recognition of God. But mother and father exist for us, have a presence inside us which remains beyond the immediate moment of physical recognition and likewise God should exist for us beyond the moments of formal prayer, worship and liturgy. Just as the physical encounter with parents intensifies the realisation of their existence, so formal prayer, worship and liturgy act as intensifying moments for God's presence which in the Catholic tradition has been reinforced by the theology of the sacraments, the mass and the real presence all of which are for me part of what I consider the essentials of the Christian tradition. To ignore, dismiss or minimise these moments is to remove a psychological reality of outstanding significance which of course has a theological reality of equal significance. The serious error that has been made is to concentrate on those moments and therefore fragment what should be a continuous experience of God. As a result of this mistake the whole spiritual life of the Church has had the catastrophic division of time for church and prayer and times for other activities which has had the serious repercussions of assessing the quality of Christian life by the criterion of fulfilling spiritual timetables. Nothing could be further from the truth.

When I speak about this point sooner or later people gaze at me with utter amazement as if to say – 'But surely you can't expect us to be in continuous contact with God; that's for saints, mystics and such like. If we go to church and say our prayers, that's enough, isn't it?' The answer is yes and no. Yes, we have to have these moments of special encounter with God but, like the physical contact with our parents, these are moments in a continuing awareness and it is the continuing awareness which is what the Christian aims for and I believe that the whole of our approach has to alter to achieve this. This sense of continuing awareness is not something which only saints and mystics achieve, it is the task of each one of us.

Do we lose our awareness of our parents in their physical absence? Certainly not and the reason for this is that the affective communication remains within us.

Personal Significance through Acceptance:

Beyond physical recognition there exists another type of recognition, namely that of our personal significance. In the course of our development we receive from our parents the feeling of being wanted by them. Everyone has the joy of the feeling of being wanted and the pangs of feeling rejected and, indeed, acceptance and rejection play a central role in the whole history of the relationship between God and man, as indeed it plays an overwhelming part in all our lives.

We receive the feeling of being wanted by our parents through innumerable emotional and physical signs and gestures. Through these we learn whether our presence is welcomed or not. Our security depends on this feeling of being wanted from which arises the sense of belonging. The psychological sciences are strongly demonstrating the epic struggles in our psyche which surround this sense of feeling wanted and accepted. Establishing and maintaining this feeling is a continuing source of struggle throughout our lives and, of course, plays a significant part in our life of prayer. If our sense of feeling wanted and accepted is strong and is based on authentic experience, we have a continuing closeness and awareness of our parents in their absence, because the bonds that link are now part of an emotional, feeling relationship that is no longer directly dependent on physical presence.

The feeling of being wanted by God has to be established on the same basis through prayer. Here we encounter several psychological problems. We do not have the physical infrastructure of our human contact. Even more important we do not have regular access to a human exchange which gives us emotional confirmation or denial of our state of acceptability.

In a sense this is what we have tried to achieve spiritually by developing the sense of sin. The awareness of sin is man's criterion of experience regarding acceptance or rejection by God. Prayer and the sacraments, particularly the sacrament of confession, have been used as the means of reconciliation when we feel estranged from God. The difficulty here is that in our human relationship the feeling of acceptance is a strong, vivid one, constantly reinforced, stemming from the physical intimacy of gestation and the early years, whereas the establishment of the relationship with God through baptism is an event which psychologically just does not register at all, if performed in the first few weeks of life. The implications of adult baptism will take us too far away from our subject but the analogy can be seen clearly.

Furthermore, the sense of sin which concentrates so much on the feelings of badness is a negative signalling system, whereas that between ourselves and our parents – bad relationships apart – is a positive one in which the sense of acceptance is only intermittently – and for short periods – interrupted by the feeling of disapproval and rejection. Even here distinction has to be made between disapproval and rejection, in the sense that security gives us a guaranteed sense of acceptance even if we are temporarily out of favour. In this connection I welcome the movement away from the distractions of venial and mortal sin which, whatever theological advantages they may have had, have immense psychological objections if they give the feeling that one's relationship with God is ever in a state of total severance.

Personal Significance through Appreciation:

The significance we receive from our parents through the feeling of acceptance establishes inside us a personal meaning which we have in our relationships with them and which we retain in their absence. But this personal meaning can be simply a bond of kinship, of affinity, a social significance. The Bible which describes life in the Middle East is full of genealogies. People in that part of the world derive their significance from the line of descent of their parents and this affinal link had, and still has, a great importance. Even in our society ancestry has been most important. I use the words 'has been' because increasingly there is a development in young people which is playing down the role of inheritance and is concentrating on the personal characteristics of the individual giving a depth to the sense of individual identity.

Identity experienced in this way relies a great deal on the sense of our self-esteem. How good we feel? How much can we truly accept and appreciate ourselves? How much can we realise our talents?

This distinctive and gathering movement in contemporary man is part of what I perceive to be a momentous change in man's consciousness of himself and has enormous implications for Christianity. If the relationship between man and God concentrates on the sense of sin, that is to say, staying in or out of God's good books, then a lot of our energy is consumed examining our conscience and making sure that we feel accepted by God.

I believe that beyond acceptance there exists the sense of personal significance in terms of our own goodness, our ability to feel good, lovable, worthy. This, of course, reflects not merely the acceptance we receive from our parents but the quality of appreciation which reflects their ability to affirm our progressive realisation of our potential as people in our own right.

This mutuality of recognition, acceptance and appreciation which we receive from our parents establishes our awareness of them and through them of ourselves. Technically, and the words are horrible, they become internalised objects who really live inside us continuously in their absence and after their death. The same applies to other intimate relationships as well and, of course, prayer is one of the principal means of establishing this reality with God which aims to give us a continuing awareness of God through time.

I should add here that I am not mentioning in this article a whole host of psychological features such as aspects of the personality

117

involving extroversion, introversion, neuroticism, the ability to register, retain and express feelings, span of concentration, toleration of closeness, all of which influence our individual make-up and therefore the quality of our relationship. For that we would have to delve into questions of the abnormal which is not my intention in this paper.

Intellectual Development:

Those who have been following my argument closely will have noted that I have said a great deal about feelings and not enough about communicating with God with our minds which, after all, involves our capacity to think, reflect and reason. My answer would be unequivocal here. Certainly these are important human characteristics for communication but I do not consider them to be of vital importance in the quality of relationship. It is a fact that intelligent people have no particular monopoly of initiating and maintaining good relationships with man or with God. Our intellectual assets are invaluable tools of human communication but they are not the principal ingredients out of which relationships are formed. It is the physical and emotional mode of communication that establishes and maintains relationships based on mutual trust, acceptance, and appreciation which are closely linked with the virtues of faith, hope and love, relating faith to trust, hope to the certainty and ultimate acceptance by God and love by Him.

Parent-Child Relationship:

From what has been said it can be seen that I have drawn a close parallel between the relationship of child and parent and that between man and God and, indeed, this is what I believe to be the case. Our parents act as the physical foundations through which the meaning of relationship is established and this experience is transferred to the reality of God.

A great deal of prayer based on petition, requests for guidance, thanksgiving and mediation is a direct continuation of human experiences first learned in our relationship with our parents. But in saying this I am reaching a vital and concluding phase of this first paper.

What is vital is to realize that God is far more than a parental figure. His own reality is a revealed mystery which exists quite independently of what we know and understand of human parenthood. If we do not perceive this clearly, we are simply extending the anthropomorphism of the ages a bit longer.

Freud noticed this and made one of the most powerful attacks on theism that has ever taken place. In *The Future of an Illusion* the writes about the origins of religious ideas thus:-

'These, which are given as teachings, are not precipitates of experience, or end results of thinking; they are illusions, fulfilments of the oldest, strongest and most urgent wishes of mankind. The secret of their strength lies in the strength of these wishes. As we already know, the terrifying impressions of helplessness in childhood aroused the need for protection – for protection through love – which was provided by the father; and the recognition that this helplessness lasts throughout life made it necessary to cling to the existence of a father, but this time a more powerful one. Thus the benevolent rule of a divine Providence allays our fears of the dangers of life.'

What Freud is saying is that we project our earthly father into a heavenly one because of our sense of helplessness and need for protection. Clearly he is describing one of the central psychological aspects of religion for, although he is wrong in the sense that God exists, and intervenes in man's affairs other than as a protector and has meaning far beyond fatherhood, there is no doubt that in practice we have treated God exactly as Freud claimed.

This is seen in the increasing debates about God meeting our needs and answering our prayers, as if his reality depended on a clear response to our needs which are answered. The same applies to the question of suffering. How could God who is loving and caring allow suffering? In my view all these issues which occupy a substantial part of prayer in our ordinary lives are both irrelevant and wrong questions even though most understandable in the light of our treating God as a fatherly protector. But the implications of these questions are massive for the life of faith. To the extent that God is seen as a parental provider and protector then clearly his validity for us depends whether he fulfils this role. If he does, we have a sense of justification, if not a sense of disappointment, a severe test of faith and ultimately its loss, for, to put it the way the majority of people see it, such a God is a fake.

So we come back to the question – What is our experience of this relationship with God, for only when we have this right will our communication through prayer be right.

Here we have to return to the child-parent model and see it in its development. By the end of the second decade a separate person has emerged with a sense of acceptance, appreciation and self esteem which has been made the basis of their self image. A separate identity has been forged which relates to the parents and to others on a basis of personal equality. The young man or woman has now to exist on his own, no longer dependent for survival through the active intervention of parents. From now on he or she is one self-contained person, the parents another, each respecting the other's freedom and independence but having a continuing awareness of each other, a continuous relationship of love.

119

What happens in the individual relationship in the family, happens between man and God, in and through Christ. Christ has this relationship of Sonship but, at the same time, of utter equality with the Father and each one of us approaches the Father through our identification with Christ.

God becomes for us the most significant 'Other', just as our parents will always remain the most significant 'Other' in our lives in the sense of having given and nurtured life. In the same way God remains the significant other with whom we have a continuous relationship, an awareness that extends well beyond petitions, requests, need for sustenance, thanksgiving. All this has to go on because it is in our nature but the awareness of God transcends all this and never depends on an outcome, *for the real development of the relationship reaches the point where the awareness of the 'Other' is all that matters.*

As far as our own life is concerned, we plot a course based on this awareness and this is where prayer is really vital for it is the means of retaining this awareness, this communication. The contents are of secondary importance always. But if we are steeped in an awareness of God then this gives us a clarity, a confidence in the meaning and purpose of our life which sustains us through failure and disappointment, gives us encouragement and hope and reassurance when things are going well.

Prayer is a means of continuing and strengthening this awareness which in fact makes a fantastic difference to the life of an individual and shapes all motivation in accordance with it.

But this is no longer the prayer of a child whose survival depends on a demonstration of active physical or emotional parental response. God may or may not answer our petitions, he may or may not allow us to suffer, he may or may not allow us to be successful. His presence does not depend on our daily state and the sooner this is realised the better.

We are utterly free, independent and responsible for our own lives. But this life is shaped, moment by moment, through an awareness of the 'Significant Other' who gives meaning to our reality. Prayer in whatever form is the means of maintaining this awareness. It can be verbal or silent; it can be contemplative; it can be all sorts of things to suit the individual concerned. It can be short; it can be long, depending on the individual's span of concentration. It does not really matter. Its meaning is not primarily derived from its shape or content. Its meaning is primarily derived from the continuing awareness of a 'Significant Other' whose reality is love and who has revealed his intention of retaining a relationship of love with each one of us until the end of time. And it is with this one-to-one relationship that I conclude this essay, leaving for consideration the sharing of this experience with others.

PSYCHOLOGY OF PRAYER II

In the previous essay I drew attention to the critical element of prayer, namely that it is a vital form of communication between the individual and God in a process which focuses and enhances an awareness of the 'Significant Other' as a continuous experience in our lives. I pointed out the danger of allotting times of prayer which would concentrate on the communication with God but would not carry this awareness beyond that moment, thus fragmenting the spiritual experience. Instead I focused on the importance of looking at formal moments of prayer as intensified encounters within a continuous process of awareness.

This awareness is often a communal event since worship, liturgy and prayer are often carried out with other people. What is the psychological meaning of this community event?

Man in Community

The simplest answer is, of course, that each one of us belongs to a community, that of the family, the religious community, the parish, a national or international organisation and that the relationship of the community to God is expressed in the public social setting. Here indeed we have another important issue involving man's changing awareness of himself. In the past a tribe, a nation, a large community had a much greater importance than the individuals who made it up and so the communal prayer was of central significance compared to that of the individual. In the Old Testament God made his covenant with His people, with Israel, with a nation, and he intervened in the history of his people. In a different context religious life placed, until recently, a great deal of emphasis on the scrupulous attendance of community prayer. Opposed to this trend is the emergence of autonomy of nations and individuals to an unprecedented degree and in religious life also there has been tension between those who evaluated the righteousness of a religious by his or her firm adherence to community events rather than the individual exercise of prayer.

There is thus a growth of individuality which is part of man's changing sense of personal awareness which cannot be ignored and we can only do justice to it if we register this change accurately. But does this imply that the sense of community must die, must be destroyed?

Not at all. Community prayer in the parish, at home, in religious life has its own psychological validity. When people gather together there emerges the identity of a group which is an extremely powerful source of strength. By doing things together, singing, articulating, gesturing, using silence, movements of the body, we share, affirm, strengthen our own individual sense of awareness. We reinforce the feeling of identity and the sense of belonging. But there are several dangers as well.

Firstly, the sense of cohesion and identity, which such a communal activity gives, can make the group inward looking, isolated, frightened to make contact with others and their way of life and the result is the division into the 'we' and 'they.' The Catholic Church has paid a great price for its insularity, but even worse such isolation is incompatible with Christianity. Christianity is a faith of love and love by definition requires a relationship with others. Much of the contempt which is directed towards the Churches is the denial of this in their division and the innumerable historical moments when the antagonism between one Christian group and another has led to massive and bloody wars, cruelty and the denial of the principles of love. Thus the unity of the group must not run the risk of destroying the outsider, the deviant, the innovator and this is something which religious life must implement in practice when habits of prayer have to alter to accommodate the growing individualism of some members.

The second danger is that of routine and ritual. Rituals are responsible for a prescribed order of events and psychologically speaking they become a learned sequence which gradually assumes an automatic, reflex response. If we consider for a moment the liturgy and life of prayer, we can see how much of it is made up of this reflex activity through which we sit, stand up, respond, sing, etc. Now, in fact, we could not live our lives without such rituals. We simply cannot initiate daily, or at regular times, fresh or new means of carrying on the essentials of life. We all know the disturbance that the recent changes in liturgy have proved to be and yet the danger is that the ritual will fall short of a conscious, feeling, personal involvement with God. Nothing is more dangerous than the sense of spiritual fullness which we experience when we have gone through a particular sequence, involving us automatically in a whole range of familiar actions and emotions and yet it has left the core of our personality untouched. In saying this I am saying nothing new but I am drawing attention to the benefits that will accrue from the attack on the slavish attendance to routine which was a yardstick of perfection of the past.

The third danger is that a community in action through prayer or liturgy must be aware that it is a Christian community, not just an ordinary assembly of shareholders, a football crowd, lecture hall attendance or a bingo club. In other words the Christian community cannot do justice to its name unless those who form it are sufficiently aware of each other to respond with love to their presence. Nothing is less

122

Christian than the Christian community which comes together to recognize and respond to God in love without recognizing and responding to each other likewise. This is a point that affects the religious life greatly. The recent climate of personal seclusion, lack of emphasis on personal relationships, taboos on feelings, leads to a contradiction between the spirit of prayer which aims at an awareness of God who is love and the ability to love each other in the community. This is, in my view, one of the principal reasons for many departures from religious life and its resolution must become absolutely central in this period of renewal.

In fact prayer in community which does not lead to a greater awareness and affective availability to our neighbour contributes to a pseudo-mutuality which must become the focus of examination in every religious community, in every parish, indeed in the whole life of the Church and I devote this second paper to this issue.

Man in Relationship with Man:

By pseudo-mutuality I mean that we join with our neighbour in activities of prayer, worship, liturgy which are meant to be both a recognition and an awareness of God while we do not follow the other consequences of this, which is to love our neighbour in whom we shall find Christ.

Sometimes one sees a discussion of prayer which attempts to create an artificial division between personal prayer and the prayer of activity. The argument runs that in recent times the importance of prayer through work has been over-emphasized and that such an approach is insufficient. While it is true, the argument runs, that we can reach Christ in our neighbour through work, this is no substitute for personal prayer.

I believe that such argumentation is riddled with confusion. Of course it is true that we find Christ in our neighbour, this much the Gospels made absolutely clear. Perhaps the passage in Matthew regarding the last judgement shows this most clearly:

'When the Son of Man comes in his glory, escorted by all the angels, then he will take his seat on his throne of glory. All the nations will be assembled before him and he will separate men one from another as the shepherd separated sheep from goats. He will place the sheep on his right hand and the goats on his left. Then the King will say to those on his right hand – "Come, you whom my Father has blessed, take for your heritage the kingdom proposed for you since the foundation of the world. For I was hungry and you gave me food: I was thirsty and you gave me drink: I was a stranger and you made me welcome: naked and you clothed me; sick and you visited me; in prison and you came to see me." Then the virtuous will say to him in reply – "Lord, when did we see you hungry and fed you; or thirsty and gave you drink? When did we see you a stranger and made you welcome; naked and clothe you; sick or in prison and go to see you?" And the King will answer – "I tell you solemnly, in so far as you did this to one of the least of these brothers of mine, you did it to me'.

Matthew 25: 31-40

There can be no argument that we find Christ in our neighbour and therefore communication with him or her is prayer. Once again you note that I have used the word communication rather than work or doing things for our neighbour since the way we reach one another makes a profound difference to the nature of our communication and so to think of prayer in terms of work alone, without considering in depth the quality of the impact we have on another person, is a very poor foundation for real prayer.

But even allowing for the presence of prayer in the communication with our neighbour, prayer must never be torn asunder by dividing it into a personal, vertical communication with God and a horizontal one with our neighbour. These words vertical and horizontal have become extremely fashionable nowadays and, although useful to a point, they run the risk of fragmenting man and his awareness of God.

At the risk of being repetitive I would like to emphasize that prayer is a reflection of man's awareness of God, that the goal is a continuity of awareness which may receive its reinforcement from the personal communication with God or with our neighbour and this is a two way exchange that forms one dynamic whole.

If I can take a moment for a personal remark: I am often asked how I can square my profession as a psychiatrist with being a Catholic or a Christian. My reply is always that I don't separate my work and my sense of myself. I am me and this awareness of myself has as its infrastructure the awareness of God in and through Jesus Christ that forms the basis of all my motivation minute by minute. In this sense, every second is a life of prayer because I cannot separate one moment of my work from my continuous awareness of my neighbour as the Christ to whom I have to respond with my being through a living acknowledgement. In this state there is no question of thinking about my Catholicity or about my Christianity; these are an essential part of my being in relationship to myself and every other person. Nor is there really room for formal examination of conscience, since every moment makes the gap between the desired and the actual love exchanged, an eternity of suffering or fulfilment in God's presence.

Such a unity of conscious awareness and action is, I believe, what the life of prayer is about. Relationship with one's neighbour which has no conscious sense of God through Christ is by definition humanism and it forms the answer to the endless questions raised nowadays about what differentiates the good humanist from the Christian. It is simply the awareness of God and the motivation that flows from it.

But, at this point, many – very many – will point to the yawning gap between the Christian ideal of love and the appalling performance of this and, of course, they would be right; so let us look at this discrepancy at this point in time with psychology as the background to our examination.

Beyond Physical Needs:

In the Matthew text I have just quoted, Christ was referring to hunger, thirst, nakedness, imprisonment, estrangement. These are a combination of material and social needs with which Christianity has always been concerned and the history of the last century of religious life would be a testimonial to the heed taken of these instructions. Clearly meeting Christ in such a needy person is prayer but there are a number of questions that need to be pursued in this area.

The first one concerns the changing social climate in developed countries where the manifestations of these acute forms of material deprivation are receding. This is not to say that there are no pockets of poverty which are still marked, simply that the conscience of society has made the excesses of these problems less pronounced. Nevertheless, the fact that the state has taken over these responsibilities does not mean that there is nothing left for others to do. Far from it; there is always going to be room for voluntary organisations, even if the character of work may change.

The second point, which is crystal clear to me as a psychiatrist, is that deprivation is not in fact a matter of physical needs alone. Social and psychological deprivation in the form of colour and race prejudice, social inequality and injustice and personality disorder responsible for suicidal attempts, alcoholism, sexual deviations, marital breakdown, childhood behaviour disturbance, some forms of delinquency, lack of realisation of potential, adolescence disorders, drug addiction, promiscuity, etc., all form a whole new cluster of needs belonging to those whom I have called the New Poor. There is work here to keep us busy for a very long time.

Quality of Personal Relationship:

Yet another important aspect in the change-over from meeting physical to psychological needs is the question of the relationship between giver and receiver. This meeting point forms another critical

125

part of the change in man's consciousness of himself. An ever deepening recognition of the significance of our neighbour demands that, whatever point of contact we make, we must treat him with the care, dignity and love that is appropriate to the spiritual reality of making contact with Christ. No psychology of prayer can escape this mystery.

Here I believe that the theology of the sacraments, which have so obviously defined the specific encounter between ourselves and Christ, have also limited and narrowed down our conscious awareness that the Church is Christ, is the sacrament which allows a perpetual encounter between ourselves and Christ at each and every moment we make contact with another person. Naturally the quality of this encounter is of vital significance to the meaning of prayer.

We can feed the hungry, clothe the naked, welcome the stranger, visit the prisoner and remain totally aloof from really loving that person. Instead we see someone whose material or social needs have been met through our intervention. If we are not careful, the whole exchange gives meaning to our life because of the very fact that we were the givers and the other person the receiver. Psychologically such a situation arouses interest in us so long as we feel needed and received on our terms but, in fact, love requires that we approach the other person on a basis of total equality. They are not naked and we clothed, hungry and we replete, imprisoned and we law-abiding, strangers and we safe in our community. Each and every one of these is Christ and our encounter is with Christ who is hungry, naked, estranged, thirsty, imprisoned.

This means that we have to become aware of those we serve as people in their own right who can disagree, reject, repudiate, stand up for themselves, not be grateful and, to the extent we are allowed, we have to remain in a relationship of service and love with them. A hard thing to do but an absolutely necessary one when the exchange is no longer seen on the external appearance of inequality, in terms of what we have and they do not, but rather of an encounter between two persons loving and sharing the reality of Christ in each other.

This, of course, appertains to all the work that has been referred to. Yes, it is true that the state can look after the materially deprived but the quality of the relationship, of course, must always be the criterion of love. This is not to say that only Christians have the prerogative of treating others with these refinements of loving. Not at all, but it does imply that the person who relates in and through Christ has a mandatory obligation to shape his relationship according to the existing principles of the fullest realisation of love in personal relationship.

The quality of the personal relationship depends, of course, a great deal on the psychological exchange taking place between people in what has been described as a relationship of love.

Relationship of Love:

a) Recognition

Perhaps the first point to examine here is the conscious level of recognition of the other person. If a person is hungry, how much more of that person do we recognize than their hunger? If a person is talking to us, how much more of that person do we recognize beyond the words and thoughts that are being exchanged? If two people are physically in touch with one another, how much of the other person is recognized beyond the physical encounter? Beyond body and intellect, how much of the feeling world of another person do we recognize?

When we talk of love we are talking about the wholeness of the other person. How much of it do we recognize? With how much of our own wholeness? How accurately do we recognize it? How accurately do we respond to it? Please note that I did not write — how fully do we respond to it, because the limitations of effective response are not a lack of loving, provided we are aware fully of the other person, and they of us, and we strive towards a fuller exchange. Just as the love of God is not to be judged by his immediate response but by the certainty of his awareness of us, so the first experience of love is getting the feel that another person is sufficiently conscious of our presence.

Everyday language would use here the word understand. We speak of understanding each other. But the sense of recognizing another person socially, physically, emotionally precedes that of our understanding them. And in any case, if understanding is confined to one dimension, say the intellectual, then certainly people who exchange thoughts are not necessarily recognizing each other as whole people. Just as the person who is communicating exclusively physically — such as the promiscuous individual — he or she is certainly not recognising the other person as a whole person. The person who is simply living on spontaneous discharge of emotion, be it anger, fear or pleasure is also unaware of the feelings of the other person. Of course the lack of recognition of the other person often corresponds to those parts of ourselves which we do not register fully and therefore cannot be conscious of in the other.

So initiating a relationship depends on how much of another person we can recognize, how accurate and how effective we are in our declaration of this recognition. We can all recollect occasions in our lives when we felt that we simply did not mean anything, or certainly enough, to another person or when we knew that the way we were treated did not reflect accurately our own sense of ourselves. This latter point is of particular importance in community life in the relationship between the superior and other members of the community for, in a special way, he or she represents God. If in fact they are incapable of

127

doing justice to the correct recognition of another person, then there is a potentially disastrous situation.

Love in Relationship:

b) Affirmation

Thus relationships of love require the growing ability to recognize accurately the wholeness of the other person which means their social, physical, intellectual and emotional needs. This appropriate recognition is the basis of initiating a voluntary relationship. I use the word voluntary because it emphasizes the importance of freedom and the absence of fear in authentic relationships of love. So many of us find ourselves in contact with other people, for a variety of reasons, without having chosen them or they us. We cannot consider the possibility of love until there is a freely chosen movement in their direction and this applies distinctly in community life. A husband chooses his wife and vice versa; a religious chooses a particular congregation but not the individuals in it. There has to grow a personal link which is freely chosen. Communities have to go on examining how many of the members present have really taken this step of voluntary exploration of the full recognition of others and how much pseudo-mutuality there exists. This, of course, not only applies to religious life but to every group of people who come together in various degrees of lack of personal choice.

I have written in the past about the contradiction in the life of the Church, which should be a life of love, but is often a loveless reality. One aspect of this is the operation of freedom in the relationships which exist inside the Church. The election of officials is one such framework of reference and the extension of freedom of selection which has generated so much tension, as in the case of bishops and the Pope, is for me a question of love. To the extent there is greater participation of the laity and priests in all such elections, there is far more involved than the introduction of a democratic process, instead there is a little bit more of the possibility of freedom which is another foundation of love.

The second point apart from freedom is the absence of fear. So many relationships exist on the basis of fear, bringing about a compliance which in authoritarian systems, such as the ones which have recently existed within the Church, is incompatible with love. Here I should like to quote further from John, this time from his famous First Epistle which confirms the point of prayer in personal encounters and the need to eradicate fear.

No one has ever seen God
but as long as we love one another

128

God will live in us
and his love will be complete in us.
We can know that we are living in him
and he is living in us
because he lets us share his Spirit.
We ourselves saw and we testify
that the Father sent his Son
as Saviour of the world.
If anyone acknowledges that Jesus is the Son of God,
God lives in him, and he in God.
We ourselves love him and put our faith in
God's love towards ourselves.
God is love
and anyone who lives in love lives in God,
and God lives in him.
Love will come to its perfection in us
when we can face the day of Judgement without fear;
because even in this world
we have become as he is.
In love there can be no fear
but fear is driven out by perfect love,
because to fear is to expect punishment,
and anyone who is afraid is still imperfect in love.

1 John 4. 12-18.

Once we initiate a relationship which aims to recognize as much of
the wholeness of another person, based on a mutual exchange of
personal freedom and absence of fear, the challenge is its continuation.

In doing this, it has to be recognized that no relationship begins on
the basis of total freedom or absence of fear. Even if there are no
external constraints, there are internal ones, not least that our motivation is up to a point a prisoner of our past, both individual and that
of our cultural setting. Furthermore, there are in all of us fears of
exposing ourselves to others and they to us. These fears may be
marked, such as in those who have pronounced feelings of inferiority,
or less marked, but all the progress to closeness and intimacy requires
the ability to diminish fear and increase the positive sense of ourselves.

This is a process of affirmation which we are all expecting from
those with whom we have an authentic relationship. John can say
unequivocally that he knows God lives in him, he obviously felt that his
personality was affirmed by God's presence. This is precisely what we
need from each other, to feel confirmed and affirmed in our own
humanity. Those of you who have followed my particular line of
thought will know that I am getting close here to an issue to which I

129

attach particular importance and have referred to before.

In our traditional Christian background there has been enormous emphasis attached to the sense of sin, badness, guilt feeling, conversion, change for the better. Personal growth is seen via the eradication of our weak, defective bad points. This is certainly an important part of growth but in my opinion not the principal one. Instead there has to be an emphasis on the positive expansion of the gifts, talents, goodness of each one of us: an affirmation of the certainty that we are lovable which is what John is referring to.

Affirmation, the process of identifying, bringing out, reinforcing the goodness of another person is essential for the continuation of a relationship. In a sense the other person depends on us to see characteristics in them which they are not conscious of and to render them available to them, as we expect them to do this to us. Of course it is easier to recognize the things which annoy us and to believe that we are helping them to grow by pointing out their weaknesses. This in my view achieves often precisely the opposite result, by confirming the other person's sense of defect, weakness and badness.

Instead the proper balance is always to place affirmation as the principal means of communication and, having created an atmosphere of trust, acceptance and encouragement, then the defects can be shown but not in an exaggerated way and certainly not as the principal route to further personal growth. There are enormous implications here for the sacrament of penance but this would take us away from the main theme.

Love in Relationship:

c) Negotiation of conflict

Authentic relationships exist when we recognise as many dimensions as possible in the other person and learn how to affirm appropriately the various growing points of each of them in another person, as indeed they should be doing with us. The depth of this communication will vary from relationship to relationship but in order to talk of love, some of these characteristics have to be present and maintained.

Now the continuation of a relationship must of necessity also be able to negotiate conflict. Others have the capacity to hurt us and we are likewise likely to do the same. This hurt can take the form of misunderstanding, misconstruing, rejecting, devaluing, repudiating, negating, refusing, attacking, etc. Forgiveness is an integral and vital element of Christian life and it is also a process which has been greatly illuminated by the psychological sciences.

Sufficient to say that forgiveness and reconciliation belong to the presence of authentic relationships of love and the metanoia or change of heart, familiar to Christians, is intimately related to the psychological process of self understanding and changing patterns of behaviour which have to follow psychological rules. These rules are related to the growing sense of personal freedom acquired in the process of losing immature habits and acquiring a greater feeling of possession of ourselves in a way that the positive acceptance of ourselves is greater than the negative, rejecting element. In other words we are much less threatened by others the more we can find within ourselves the sources of our acceptance.

Thus every hurt we receive and give should prompt us to reflect on what part of us needs strengthening and, as far as authentic relationships of love are concerned, beyond forgiveness there must be an attempt at healing and restoring the missing or defective component of the personality. For this we need the loving care of others who can give us a deeper insight into ourselves in a spirit of positive growth, rather than a confrontation of our badness.

In fact we need very much the assistance of those who care for us to strengthen our inner resources to avoid temptation. If they love us, they will help us by minimising the stress we are subjected to and we do likewise to them. This is done by giving a friendly warning in good time and not using weaknesses as a way to lord it over each other, defects to maintain a superior-inferior position, or a sense of guilt as a means of blackmailing others into action to our advantage.

Recognition, affirmation, reconciliation, healing, growth are some of the principal ingredients of love in personal relationships and, of course, the test of love is how long we can maintain such a relationship when the other person is not able to reciprocate or is actively attacking us.

The answer is in the Old Testament which is a history of repudiation by the people of God and fidelity on the part of Yahweh and this remains the same with Christ whose love for us has become the body of the Church in which we participate through baptism and is reinforced most actively through the Eucharist. It is a relationship that has no end and, to the extent we try to imitate this in every one of our own relationships, we are praying, by relating to Christ in our neighbour as he relates to us in our lives.

The effort to maintain our relationships of love in the face of the various human difficulties of separation, desertion, misunderstanding, conflict, loss of mutual interest, lack of mutual fulfilment is an active expression of faith which is sustained by the constant awareness of God through Christ and it completes the unity of prayer which I have tried to express in these two papers.

But there is even a more fitting completion in the Lord's Prayer which I believe is expressing these same ideas. In Matthew we have the following text:

'Our Father in heaven,
May you name be held holy,
your kingdom come,
your will be done
on earth as in heaven;
Give us to-day our daily bread
And forgive us our debts
as we have forgiven those who are in debt to us.
And do not put us to the test,
but save us from the evil one.

'Yes, if you forgive others their failings, your heavenly Father will forgive you yours; but if you do not forgive others, your Father will not forgive your failings either.'

Matt. 6. 7-15.

If you study the text carefully you will see that the first half of the prayer draws our attention to the existence of God the Father and requires us to form a relationship with him. If you like, this is the vertical relationship, the personal, one-to-one encounter in which we learn the characteristics of our Father, just as we had to learn the characteristics of our earthly parents.

Halfway through, our awareness of God brings him in our midst, when his will will be done on earth as it is in heaven. And on earth the implementation of his will requires us to be in relationship with others which will make it possible to keep us alive by fulfilling our needs, resolving our conflicts in love and helping us directly and through others to overcome evil.

The Lord's Prayer is the perfect example of that unity, of awareness of God which provides our inner link with him, minute by minute, who is living in our relationships of love with each other which are sustained by the consciousness of his presence.

PART IV

In the penultimate part, the two essays return in a way back to the initial one. They were given at King's College, London and to a conference of lay married people respectively. These essays start with an examination of human and divine love and continue with an examination of love in death, for a Christian the conclusion of one life and the beginning of another. The first essay 'Facing Death' was published in *Matters of Life and Death* (Darton, Longman & Todd, 1970) and is re-printed here for the sake of completion in our consideration of the whole human cycle.

FACING DEATH

The theme of this essay has developed slowly. Some few years ago I was treating an intelligent man, in his early thirties who was morbidly preoccupied with death, his own pending disintegration. He was an anxious person who suffered a great deal from these recurrent fears. At this stage of the proceedings I remembered thinking about Christ and his attitude to death. I suppose the similarity of age had something to do with this but I did not pursue it any further.

This patient was not however an isolated example of patients preoccupied with fears of death. Men and women of all ages, but particularly in their teens, twenties and thirties come repeatedly to my clinic complaining spontaneously of these feelings. Eventually I began to ask myself about such fears and little by little a clinical picture emerged. These men and women had certain features in common. They were frequently of an anxious disposition. This could well be ascribed to their constitutional make up and related to genetic influences. With persistent uniformity they lacked a clear sense of their personal identity.

Coupled with this absence of a clear identity is a recurrent fear of a personal disintegration of annihilation expressed in such terms of depersonalisation as: 'I fear that something terrible will happen' or 'nothing would be left of me'. Intimately associated with these feelings is the dread of the unknown, up or down there in pre-Bishop of Woolwich language, and the terror of leaving behind the objects and people who are sources of comfort and support.

This personality structure and feelings are a frequent clinical picture and as the numbers I saw increased I thought again about Christ. His approach to death was at the opposite pole of this continuum. It could be said that he almost looked forward to it. He certainly spoke about it with equanimity and sombre anticipation.

Mark writes 'And he began to teach them that the Son of Man was destined to suffer grieviously, to be rejected by the elders and the chief priests and the scribes and to be put to death, and after three days to rise again and he said all this quite openly'. 8:31.

In John 10:14 we find 'I am the good shepherd, I know my own and my own know me, just as the Father knows me and I know the Father and I lay down my life for my sheep'.

In John 13: 19 'I tell you this now, before it happens so that when it does happen you may believe that I am He.'

In Mark 9: 31 'The Son of Man will be delivered into the hands of men; they will put him to death and three days after he has been put to death he will rise again'.

These and other passages exemplify our Lord's calm anticipation of the central event in his life. There was no fear of the unknown. He knew he was going to the Father and there was no terror of leaving behind those with whom he was related.

By now a theme was developing in my mind. Such a clear cut view of death handled with such little disturbance presupposes, if my view is correct, a strong and definitive identity.

I am well aware of the danger of looking for what one wants in the Scriptures to support a particular point of view. The texts povide an abundance of material which can be variously interpreted. There is, however, indisputable evidence indicating that Christ possessed an identity which showed the characteristics of certainty, security, self acceptance and an overwhelming capacity to love and be loved.

Long before his ministry started Christ indicates his close relationship to the Father and it is in this intimate union that he finds and expresses most clearly his own identity as a beloved Son with a specific mission. Here we are in the midst of the mystery of the Incarnation. We know little about Christ's relationship with Mary and Joseph. The references to the former are few. Such as they are they show respect, care and concern, especially at the crucifixion; but at times there is a powerful redirection of emphasis from his human situation to God the Father. The woman who raises her voice in the crowd to say 'Happy the womb that bore you and the breast you sucked' is not contradicted but the reply 'Still happier (are) those who hear the word of God and keep it' is an emphatic assertion of priorities in relationships. Again in Luke when his mother and his relations came looking for him but could not reach him the reply to those who pointed out their presence was curt. 'My mother and my brothers are those who hear the word of God and put it into practice' (Lk 8: 21). Christ does not reject his mother and his love for her is indicated in the Crucifixion narrative of St. John in which he takes care to leave her in the care of his beloved disciple. This brief episode says all that we need to know of how much he cared for her. But there is no escaping the fact that his only significant relationship was with his Father. With God the Father there is a constant dialogue in which Christ received indisputable affirmation of his identity, and the measure of love that his Father entertains for him. At his baptism there is an early affirmation. 'And a voice spoke from heaven, This is my beloved son with whom I am well pleased' (Matt 3: 17). Thus at the beginning of his messianic mission there is an unequivocal declaration of the intimate relationship between Father and Son and the total approval by the former of the work of the latter. Christ affirms that he draws his life from the Father. 'As I, who am sent by the living Father, myself draw life from the Father, so whoever eats me will draw life from me' (Jn 6: 57).

The closeness between Christ and the Father is to be seen in a number of passages particularly in the gospel of St. John. When the Pharisees questioned his integrity he showed no trepidation in his reply.

'You judge by human standards, I judge no one but if I judge, my judgement will be sound because I am not alone; the one who sent me is with me:'

(Jn 8: 15-16)

Here as in other passages there is a certainty which in any other circumstances could be interpreted as arrogance, delusion or imagination. But the certainty never varies.

'If God were your father, you would love me, since I have come here from God. Yes, I have come from him.'

(Jn 8: 42)

and again

'The Father and I are one.'

(Jn 10: 30)

or

'The Father is in me and I am the Father.'

(Jn 10: 38)

In this closeness there is the certainty of unconditional acceptance, the essential prerequisite for the secure growth and development of every person.

'As the Father has loved me,
so I have loved you.'

(Jn 15: 9)

'I tell you most solemnly anything you ask for
from the Father he will grant in my name.'

(Jn 16: 23)

These and other passages indicate Christ's utter confidence that his Father acknowledged, approved and accepted him without qualification.

He had been chosen to carry out a mission, to reconcile man to the Father. He loved the Father and he loved man and because of this love he chose freely the incarnation and the cross. But in undertaking this tremendous task he was supported by a self knowledge which could not be daunted by any human circumstances.

When the Jews became utterly impatient and sarcastic the reply is devastating.

'My glory is conferred by the Father
by the one of whom you say "He is our God"
although you do not know him.
But I know him, and if I were to say: I do not know him,
I should be a liar, as you are liars yourselves.
But I do know him, and I faithfully keep his word.
Your father Abraham rejoiced to think he could
See my Day; he saw it and was glad.'

The Jews then said 'You are not fifty yet, and
you have seen Abraham!'

Jesus replied:

'I tell you most solemnly, before Abraham ever was,
I am.'

(Jn 8:54: 58)

Psychologically this last sentence is breathtaking. The passage of time, change and the various facets of disintegration have no impact in this unique personality. 'Before Abraham ever was, I am' carries us into a concept of continuing and unchangeable indentity beyond any circumscribed human experience and an overwhelming protection against the threat of death. It is of the utmost significance to note that this categorical assertion of personal permanency is linked in this passage with the relationship to the Father. So long as Christ felt close to the Father, no threat existed to his identity and he encountered no difficulty in facing his approaching death. But his feelings of closeness were so threatened twice. I use the word feelings here purposely. Both in the Garden of Gethsemane and on the cross Christ experienced extreme emotional disturbance. Mark refers to 'sudden fear' and great distress. Matthew writes about sadness and distress and Luke describes his anguish and the sweat that fell to the ground like great drops of blood. All these descriptions in the garden are characteristic of an anxiety crisis with acute somatic manifestations and a marked mood swing towards depression. These are exactly the manifestations experienced

137

by the patients who have morbid preoccupation with death and fear personal dissolution. In Our Lord's case these symptoms emerge at the moment when there is a crisis of his identity and a threatened separation between himself and the Father. If he was to remain the person he was, he had to go on and meet his death however terrifying this prospect might suddenly have become to him. To do otherwise would have disrupted the links with the Father. This was not possible and intellectually he knew this. In John's Gospel, Christ praying to the Father at about the same time asserts unequivocally:-

'Father, may they be one in us
as you are in me and I am in you.'

(Jn 17: 21)

Intellectual certainty that he and the Father are one and the mission entrusted to him could not be denied nevertheless did not stop the emotional upheaval. This dichotomy between intellect and the will on the one hand and the emotions on the other is a recurrent feature of psychiatric work and demonstrates the absolute need to get away from the view held for so long which laid the emphasis on the intellectual and conative aspects of the human personality. There is abundant evidence to relate the emotional integrity of the individual with both the environment of his upbringing and his inheritance. As far as the environment is concerned, the threat of displeasure and consequent separation from the beloved parent is a source of great upheaval amply demonstrated by Christ who, while he knew he could not let his Father down, experienced one of his two episodes of acute emotional distress at the moment this became a possibility.

Christ, however, possessed such strong bonds with the Father, that he was able to overcome the fear and to continue in his role. The security of his relationship with the Father overcame the dread of personal disintegration and he continued with his passion.

'Father', he said, 'If you are willing, take
this cup away from me. Nevertheless, let
your will be done, not mine.'

(Lk. 22: 43)

The Father's will led to the cross where the second episode of crisis is encountered.

In Matthew's and Mark's Gospels we have identical references.

'Eli, Eli, Lama Sabachthani,
that is 'My God, my God, why have you
deserted me?'

(Mat. 27: 46-47; Mk. 15: 34)

The whole of our Lord's identity depended, as the Scriptures demonstrate beyond any shadow of doubt, on his indissoluble union of love with the Father. The feeling of desertion, of abandonment expressed by Christ on the cross, is in my opinion the most painful moment of our Lord's life. Closeness with the Father was the guarantee of his existence and at that moment Christ experienced aloneness and with it the excruciating agony of isolation. The relevance for the human personality needs no further elaboration from me. But Christ's last experience was not that of abandonment.

'Father into your hands I commit my spirit.'
With these words he breathed his last.

(Lk. 23: 46)

The words 'Into your hands I commit my spirit' come from Psalm 31.

'Pull me out of the net they have spread for me,
for you are my refuge;
into your hands I commit my spirit,
you have redeemed me, Yahweh.'

(P. 31: 4-5)

Our Lord dies with the certainty of the unuttered sentence, fulfilled in his Father.

All Christians are involved in the threefold process of creation, salvation and eschatological fulfilment and for the completion of the circle death is an inescapable reality. Only through death can we join in the triumph of the resurrection. But the life of faith has to be built on the natural order, where pain, suffering, distress are concrete experiences. The Christian preoccupation with death stands in marked contrast to an age which is consciously preoccupied with minimising by every possible means this reality. This is understandable in terms of a philosophy of life that will not entertain existence beyond the here and now. Perhaps nowhere else than at death's door do humanism and Christianity part their ways so completely. For the humanist death leaves behind a physical, social and cultural contribution which allows the continuity of the race physically and aesthetically. For the Christian death leaves behind all this but adds the Kingdom of God. Christianity has rightly emphasised the need to assist and comfort the dying and to inspire them at these critical moments with the hope and courage that will sustain their faith. The care of the dying is a field in which contemporary Christianity has a lot to contribute in this country and we owe much to the work of Dr. C. Saunders and all those who assist her. This is a task which we must continue and extend.

But as you may have guessed I want to conclude with a different concept. It would seem to me that preparation for death not only needs the right circumstances to support those about to face this event but also the promotion of an identity which allows the personality to anticipate it with the equanimity of Christ. Preparation for death starts with the right human environment in which the personality can grow securely, with the fullest possible self acceptance and a purposeful sense of direction. Only in the fullness of being human can death find an acceptance which minimises its stress. For this Christianity needs to complement its work at the time of death with attention to the time of birth and the early years of development in the family. The last half century has opened for us unparalleled avenues in which psychology has given us remarkable insights about the integrity of the human personality. It has to be admitted sadly that Christianity has been desperately slow to seize the opportunities that have now been opened to it. The tools are there for further work and research to deepen our understanding of the best conditions under which the growth of identity should take place. Christianity must become involved at both ends of life so that journey's end is accomplished with the sense of accomplishment that we see on the Cross. Death will always remain a threat to us but our ability to overcome it will depend on our ability to develop intact human personalities on which the life of faith and grace will have the maximum impact. Such thorough integration is seen in the life and approach to death of Christ. We have reached a point in history when we can make further use of the abundance of love that his life and example have given to us.

GRIEF

The traditional Catholic teaching on death interprets this moment as the final determining point in the encounter between man and God which decides each soul's eternal relationship with its creator. Hence the emphasis on leading a good life and the importance of a final repentance in case of the opposite. Death bed scenes of ultimate contrition or stubborn refusal to yield to God's mercy have played a prominent role in the spiritual and cultural heritage of the Christian West. Representations of the damned and the blessed on opposite sides have contributed to innumerable graphic and pictorial scenes which have dominated our thinking and feeling about this moment, and, like so much else of Christian life, fear has played an important part in depicting death's consequences. Fear of eternal pain and suffering as the punishment of the wicked has underpinned powerfully the message of Christianity and undoubtedly one powerful reason for its temporary decline is humanity's decreasing readiness to respond to this. Men and women accustomed to climbing Everest, reaching the moon, splitting the atom and the mystery of the genetic code are increasingly immune to the crude pictorial and verbal threats of hell fire. Furthermore, they consider that a God and a Church that indulge in such practices are not worth cultivating.

This massive indifference to the centuries-old means of communicating the Christian message has confronted the Church with a complex problem. The response to modernism on the part of the Catholic Church will be seen by historians in due course as a singularly unsuccessful attempt to stifle man's growth towards a more penetrating awareness of the meaning of God. After nearly a hundred years of frustrating, at times utterly confusing, rearguard action, the Second Vatican Council under guidance of the Spirit is offering the Church an opportunity to assess critically and incorporate the truths that man has been discovering about himself. The tensions resulting from this process are well known and appear to me to be inevitable. The price of the self inflicted wounds of hundreds of years of stagnation, lack of initiative and imagination has been heavy. The work of reconstruction has now begun and certainly, as far as I am concerned, I am happy to leave it to the historian to assess the reasons for the failure and to apportion responsibility. There is so much to do to bring Christ to the notice of our neighbour afresh that to indulge in petty internal squabbles within the

141

Church seems to be a reprehensible waste of energy.

Instead our efforts are needed for the urgent task of reconciliation with, and further exploration by, Christians of those disciplines which are giving us new and authentic insights into the nature of man.

The subject of my paper is Grief and is one which psychoanalytic thought has considered in some detail. Grief is intimately associated with the process of mourning which has been defined as 'The psychological processes that are set in train by the loss of a loved object and that commonly lead to the relinquishing of the object.' "Object" is a technical term in psychoanalytic language meaning a person and this sometimes leads to confusion. "Object" stands for the person to whom the infant forms its first attachment, before it is in a position to comprehend the significance and meaning of an adult. A great deal of psychoanalytic study has concentrated on the growing child's awareness of mother and father progressively from limited objects which meet and gratify its physical needs to whole persons with whom it relates physically, emotionally and rationally. In fact this is the correct order of developing awareness and is in contrast to traditional thinking which attached primary importance to the development of the intellectual faculties from school age onwards. These five or six pre-school years have been the subject of intense study for over threequarters of a century and the Christian neglect of their significance is one of the current impoverishments which need changing.

The roots of understanding the process of mourning will indeed be found in the events that occur during these early years and it is a process that has been examined exhaustively by one of the leading writers in this country, Dr. J. Bowlby; he has already written the first part of a two volume study called *Attachment and Loss.* This first volume deals with the processes by means of which the child forms ties with the mother and the second will deal with the consequences of losing the mother or a loved object.

What Bowlby and other psychoanalysts have been describing, from the time of Freud's first great paper on the subject "Mourning and Melancholia" in 1915, is the essential connection between mourning and the loss, temporarily or permanently, of any significant person in our lives. The most familiar loss is that ensuing from death, but physical death is anticipated during life by innumerable moments of psychological death in which we are separated from or lose someone who means a great deal to us.

The prototype of this experience is laid down in the first few years of life. Bowlby's study which collates a great deal of associated work focuses on the infant's capacity to form an attachment. This attachment is made in the overwhelming majority of cases with the mother and is mediated by a series of interrelated processes.

Now in the first three years the young child learns how to cope with actual physical separation from its mother. It is hard for adults to understand this but at this early stage of life the actual physical absence of mother from the visual and auditory field of the child is equivalent to the total loss, to psychological death, and is associated with separation anxiety. Each year the child is able to accept progressively longer periods of separation from mother without anxiety, and by the third year onwards it can cope with a separation of some hours as all nursery school teachers and parents know. What is it that allows the child to separate from mother safely?

The ability to survive loss depends on the existence of an accumulated series of experiences which make it safe for the person to survive alone. In other words the child has learned to associate safety, comfort and gratification with the presence and behaviour of the mother and is now gradually capable of internalising these feelings within itself. It needs less and less the active physical presence of the loved object to remind it of the signals and experiences of safety. It carries within itself a store of learned images, sensations and feelings which act as an internal psychological battery.

It needs of course a stable, safe and reliable early environment to accumulate these experiences from which it will gather its strength to survive alone and to cope with any subsequent loss. Strange as it may sound, the capacity to bear loss at any time subsequently in life is intimately associated with these early repeated experiences of attachment and separation.

Studies in young children under the age of three have given us information about the sequence of response to the loss of mother. First, her physical absence is reacted to with protest crying, associated with searching and seeking for her. This phase may be immediate or delayed. Normally of course mother returns soon and this brings the behaviour to an end. If she does not return, it is followed by monotonous and intermittent crying associated with detachment from toys, objects and people. There is now a mixture of hope and despair. Finally there appears a return of interest in games, food and people. At this stage everybody feels that the trauma has been healed. Unfortunately, if mother returns a few weeks later, the child is often unable to relate to her. It runs away, rejects and screams at her, an experience that mothers returning from hospital after a prolonged stay find most disconcerting. The child has to learn to form an attachment afresh. At this early stage there has not been sufficient internalisation of the familiar figure to be able to resume the intimate attachment; something which only occurs later on when the relationship has been sufficiently long and stable to allow prolonged periods of separation without interruption of the basic tie.

143

Children who have been subjected to repeated interruptions in their attachment tend to grow up with a marked defect in their ability to form close intimate relationships and equally they respond to their loss with a marked indifference. These men and women contribute to the group of men and women, called psychopaths, who portray an extreme degree of callousness in the way they form casual relationships, evoke a deep response from their partner from whom they turn away with little feeling of grief.

The normal response, the sequence of protest, despairing resignation and detachment is also the pattern for adult mourning which can now be looked at in greater detail.

The phase of protest is developed later following the feelings of denial, another technical psychological term implying a psychological refusal to accept a thought, feeling or action. It corresponds to feelings and ideas such as − 'No, it hasn't happened; it can't be; it isn't; it isn't real' or simply total denial of the event in extreme cases. Infrequently patients are admitted to a psychiatric unit who insist that their lost spouse is not dead and will meet them again shortly. Another feature of this protest-denial phase is the presence of anger, the equivalent of which is translated into such terms as − 'You can't do this to me . . . . You can't go away and leave me alone . . . . I hate you for doing this to me. . .' Death is seen by the bereaved in these circumstances as a deliberate and wilful act of hostility to those left behind. Sometimes the anger is extended to those who have looked after the person, the doctor, nurses or those who have caused any form of accident. These feelings can easily escalate to revenge. Anger may have also been felt towards the deceased as an antecedent event and the death felt as the direct consequence of these feelings. Extreme guilt can be experienced in these circumstances.

The next phase of resignation and acceptance can be truly called grief in which the person who loses their loved one can allow themselves to feel the whole extent of the pain of loss, of irretrievable loss without despair. The acute pain of physical and emotional absence is expressed and there is really no way by which this grief can be circumvented. Acute grief may last weeks or months and it is gradually replaced by a less tense pain which paves the way by a detachment which acclimatizes the individual to the physical loss. For some individuals the psychological loss is irreplaceable. They turn, however, to their internalised memories, feelings and experiences as the source of consolation and indeed their beloved lives on in a vivid and realistic manner as long as they remain alive. For others with less intense feelings, the detachment is complete physically and emotionally, and life is adapted to without the dead person, indeed a new intimate attachment is formed which may replace fully the previous one.

These feelings which are initiated in the early years of our life do not manifest themselves only at the death of our loved ones. The anxiety of separation and the grief of the loss of any close relationship, through departure or abandonment, is an equally painful process which threatens us constantly.

Whatever the source of loss, whether it be death, departure, abandonment or betrayal, the subsequent grief can be so intense that those who suffer may not wish to go on living. Suicide is not an uncommon event and indeed it has been found that widowers have an increased mortality in the first six months after their wife's death. A recent study of these widowers showed that death is very often attributable to heart disease, particulary coronary thrombosis, The age-old notion that one can die of a broken heart is perhaps not a myth. If death does not ensue during the period of bereavement a depressive illness may well supervene.

These are all the possible consequences of suffering, probably the most serious human infliction, the loss of a loved one. At the human level it is clear that there is really no protection from such an event. The only real protection, which in no way diminishes the actual anguish of the loss, is the presence of a happy and loving relationship which has given the two people ample opportunities to give each other good experiences which they can keep inside them as permanent enduring awareness, transcending the actual physical absence. Indeed, this is the only satisfactory human conclusion to any loving relationship.

This type of outcome is based on the quality and structure of the personality that suffers the loss. Such a man or woman needs to have a secure sense of their identity which can survive the loss and at the same time retain the mixture of good and bad experiences received from the deceased in a balance in which the good outweighs the bad. This in turn requires a reasonably long and satisfactory personal relationship which has allowed a rich exchange of mutually meaningful and satisfying experiences. The ability to survive the anxiety and grief of a personal loss ultimately depends on the quality of the previous relationship between the two people concerned. Although the initial loss is that much more severe for those who lose a very dear person, their ultimate ability to negotiate the loss will be much greater and more satisfactory.

The Relationship between man and God.

As far as the Christian is concerned, the People of God live in the temporal order in which we experience Christ sacramentally but live in faith with the conviction that we shall ultimately be united in him after death and re-united with all our earthly relationships in the communion of saints. This is a consoling, central tenet of our faith, even though its realisation is a mystery beyond our comprehension.

Faith is the evolving and deepening response of man to God and we can begin to see that death is much more than the moment of spiritual accountancy, more than a matching of credit and debit columns. Such crude imagery had its poignant advantages but it does little justice to the encounter between man and God which is that of an evolving relationship of closeness. In the previous essay I discussed the problem of facing death as seen by Christ's encounter with his own death. Briefly the points I made then are that Christ's approach to his own death can only be understood psychologically against a background of a totally mature identity which experienced the closest possible relationship of love with the Father. Nevertheless, even under these ideal conditions, Our Lord experienced two significant moments of acute anxiety, that is in the garden and on the cross, both associated with a temporary threat to the perfect closeness and understanding that existed between Son and Father.

The impact of our faith at the moment of death will depend clearly on the depth and the quality of our relationship with God. Faith by itself is no consolation to those who die as has been shown by the studies of Professor J. Hinton, Professor of Psychiatry at the Middlesex Hospital, London. If by faith is meant the sort of approach that concentrated on observing the externals by which "good Catholics" were distinguished from the "bad ones" then clearly it is not surprising that at the time of death, faith is of little assistance.

Faith, if it is anything, is a living contact with the Trinity in which during a life time of spiritual encounter we internalize the meaning and reality of God's revelation to man. Christ is, of course, central to this epiphany and in each age the Church will be judged by how well it has succeeded in communicating to the world the vibrant, exhilarating existence of its bridegroom. Fortified with a lifetime's internalizations, we encounter God at the moment of death in the mystery of eternity. It is a moment which utterly divides the humanist, atheist, or agnostic from the authentic believer who expects to realize, in the unseen and the unknown, a continuation of a relationship which has only just begun. The anguish of temporal and personal loss remains acute and cannot be otherwise as we witness it in our Lord, but there is also present an identification with God which retains its supreme significance for us as it did for Christ.

Christ and His Disciples

In the third and final part of this paper I would like to consider Christ's preparation of his disciples for his death and their response to it.

Our Lord had a remarkably short period to communicate himself to his apostles, a mere three years; by any ordinary human standard not unduly long to form and establish the type of relationship which allows a penetrating exchange of characteristics between people. Christ knew this and it is a reflection of the impact of his personality that this brief period had such devastating and unique consequences on his immediate disciples and thereafter on the wider community of the Church.

Our Lord knew he was going to die and told the apostles at least three times in the Gospel of Mark. In Luke, there is a poignant paragraph which follows Christ's cure of the boy suffering from convulsions.

"At a time when everyone was full of admiration for all he did, he said to His disciples: 'For your part, you must have these words constantly in your mind: The Son of Man is going to be handed over into the power of men.' But they didn't understand him when he said this.'

Luke 9: 43-45

The apostles did not understand his pending death. Why should they? They were living in the midst of a remarkable life, captivated by the teaching and actions of Christ. Losing him was as far removed from their immediate expectation as is the loss of our own dear and loved ones in the primacy of their lives. It would have been psychologically impossible to fully comprehend the significance of our Lord's warnings. But they were given nevertheless and they were received, taken in, internalized even if they remained unconscious and incomprehensible. Just as in the course of our lives the Christian message of the good news is given to us, taken in, stored in the depths of our being, internalized through faith but still remaining a mystery, an incomprehensible mystery.

All the time Christ was giving himself to the crowd and to his disciples, to the latter in a special way. His every word, action and detail of behaviour was registered, received and gradually assimilated. Our Lord knew his physical presence would be of a limited duration but the quality of the relationship was unique and the experiences he was offering to his disciples intense. The psychological significance of handing over to them previous experiences of himself which will become the essential core of their own personality afterwards is vividly and poetically portrayed in John's Gospel.

'I will not leave you orphans;
I will come back to you.
In a short time the world will no longer see me,
but you will see me,

147

> because I live and you will live;
> on that day
> you will understand that I am in my Father
> and you in me and I in you.'

John 14: 18-20

He gave himself to his apostles and they slowly took him inside them. He became part of them which they were to retain after His departure. But he did something even more significant. Just before His death he gave them wholly himself at the last supper. 'This is my body; This is my blood.' Christ gave himself completely to his disciples in an act which totally incorporated and internalized his reality in each one of his recipients, an event which is central to our own constant renewal of our own internalization of Christ.

As his departure approached, so the intensity of his own existence and his communication of self intensified. Nothing else would do to safeguard his own survival of himself than his total self which they received. The Spirit would confirm their understanding of his significance shortly but here and now he was offering himself to them and to us without this complete comprehension, just as we receive the love of husband and wife without fully appreciating immediately its meaning. Christ had no more time but he had found a unique and divine solution: he would make himself totally available on each and every occasion the event is commemorated thereafter. The pending loss on the cross is anticipated and compensated for in the last supper.

The gospels do not give clear evidence of the protest-denial, despairing resignation and detachment of the mourning process. Nor should this be expected because the event of the resurrection is still extremely close to the initial disturbing phase of Christ's death. Furthermore, the gospels cannot be comprehensive psychological documents although their authenticity must stand up repeatedly to the verifications required by our deepening understanding of human nature.

John's Gospel describes the sadness of Mary Magdalene who had now lost the body of the person she knew. Physical proximity to the dead body was being denied to her in the empty tomb. And her reaction was simply to cry. The disciples on the road to Emmaus had downcast faces. There was gloom, grief and puzzlement in those he had left behind. Their loss was not an ordinary one and their grief was mixed with a marked sense of confusion.

Christ clearly knew and understood this. He could have followed his resurrection with his ascension directly but in this unique and extraordinary situation it would not have been appropriate and so he appeared to the Apostles and in a most telling manner on the second occasion when Thomas was present. Thomas's truly human response of wanting to touch physically his hand leaves no doubt about the authenticity of the exchange. Nothing else but physical contact would have convinced him and the reply he received was not only addressed to him but the millions who would follow him to the end of time.

Jesus said to him:
'You believe because you can see me.
Happy are those who have not seen and yet believe.'

John 20: 29

"Those" are you and I and we still need Christ just as much as Thomas did. We can only find him in the Church he left behind which has internalized his reality and communicates his living reality to each one of us.

PART V

In this last essay, given at the annual conference of the Catholic Marriage Advisory Council, 1973, many of the principal ideas of all the other essays are summarised. Essentially the Christian life is based on human events, found in the family, where the chief experience needs to be that of affirmation. Human affirmation is completed by the divine affirmation which is the consummation of Christian living.

THE CYCLE OF HUMAN AFFIRMATION

On Thursday, 29th June, 1972, Sir Keith Joseph, Secretary of State for Social Services, in a major speech referred to a "Cycle of human deprivation", a theme which he returned to since elsewhere, including our own annual general conference last year.

By the "cycle of human deprivation" he has drawn the attention of a much wider public to a concept of long standing familiarity to psychiatrists, social workers and counsellors, all of whom see the adverse impact of one generation impinging on the next, who in turn fail in some crucial way to be effective in their own lives.

This lack may show itself in antisocial behaviour such as criminality, in self-damaging patterns such as alcoholism, drug addiction, suicidal attempts, suicide, work ineptitude or in less obvious aspects such as the failure to initiate or maintain personal relationships, inability to realise personal talents, educationally or later on utilise advantageously their intellectual competence or find satisfactory meaning in living. Between them these life situations involve several millions of human beings.

Even such an evocative phrase as the "cycle of human deprivation" does not, however, introduce a new concept nor is it claimed to do so. The idea that a badly endowed set of parents contribute to the impoverishment of their children is as old as the history of man. What is new, and startlingly new at that, is the view that this is not a cycle which can be dismissed by blaming, indicting or faulting the parents as if, with the responsibility placed squarely on the shoulders of somebody – father, mother or both, society had dealt with the matter, if not satisfactorily, at least logically.

This is a view that still prevails widely today. The inadequate are those who have had their opportunities and failed to take them. They are blameworthy and the gates of prison, coupled with social and moral disapproval, should – singly or in combination – open its arms to swallow all such deviancy. Sir Keith Joseph has attempted to bring finally to a close an outlook which had no alternative to shame, humiliation and punishments as the principal means for dealing with the unknown. Instead, he calls for sustained effort and research, education for parenthood; in other words, preventive work as the means of breaking the vicious circle. This has long been the conviction of all those working in this field and, now it has become government policy, I sincerely hope it will become the policy of all political parties.

Social versus Psychological Change

In his address Sir Keith referred to a paradox: namely, that despite the social changes leading to long periods of full employment, increased material prosperity, improved educational and health standards, nevertheless deprivation and problems of maladjustment persist and, in some instances, — such as, for example, marital breakdown and suicidal attempts, drug addiction in the young — appear to increase. The prophets of doom have, of course, a relatively simple answer. This, they say, is what happens when a society goes soft, when discipline becomes lax, when moral standards drop, when instinctual gratification — be it sex or aggression — goes amok. And there the argument rests, because there can be no discussion with those who have diagnosed the problem and *know* the answer.

Sir Keith refers to one answer. As the material problems recede into the background, as poverty diminishes, the social and psychological layer of existence forges into prominence. There are enough reminders that poverty is still in our midst and rife in other parts of the world. We have, nevertheless, a sober reminder that, although material deprivation is certainly an important contributor to human deprivation, its amelioration is not a guarantee for human wholeness.

As a psychiatrist this comes as no surprise and highlights one of the powerful areas of tension between psychiatry and psychology on the one hand and sociology on the other. Sociology is concerned with the social conditions of the environment; psychology with the psychological potential of the individual and the interaction between the growing organism and the environment in the principal form of the parents. No sociological utopia will ever be realised, however rich it is in material and social conditions, if the psychological opportunities are not realised in full. Sociologists, particularly of the radical school, tend to criticise the work of psychiatrists, social workers and counsellors on the grounds that they ignore the need for changes in society and simply act as agents of the prevailing establishment, whatever its nature, to make people accept, adjust and adapt to something less than they deserve. It is a criticism that we should pay heed to, but it is certainly not a reflection of the truth. For a crucial aspect of the psychological sciences is the increase in knowledge and understanding of personal growth so that deprivation is not reduced only by supplying what is missing but by expanding to the maximum the potential which is present in every individual.

Affirmation

At the other end of the scale of deprivation is affirmation which is the subject of this paper. If the family is the nucleus for the cycle of deprivation, it is also indubitably the centre for the cycle of human affirmation. The word affirmation comes from the Latin "affirmare" and it means to make firm, to give strength to. To give strength to what? To the human personality. When we think of the human personality we are, of course, prisoners of a tradition of over two and half thousand years that gave prominence to the mind, the intellect, reason, logic, with the body in the background spelling out restriction, imprisonment, instinctual danger and the world of feelings and love a constant hope, difficult to realise. In the cycle of human affirmation which I am about to consider I want, consciously and deliberately, to reverse this order. I believe the ground of being is love, at the centre of which are feelings, aided and abetted by the body and the mind, forming a whole in which all the constituent parts are important: but the moment-to-moment personal reality depends on what we feel about ourselves and others.

Identity

One of the most influential writers on the development of the human personality is the American psychoanalyst, E.H. Erikson, whose cycle of human development – described in various publications – is familiar to many of you. He attached great importance to the concept of identity, which he describes as the sense we have of ourselves and meaning for significant others, which – while altering – retains a sameness and continuity which gives an enduring awareness of ourselves. Another way of saying the same thing is by referring to two basic questions. The first one is "Who am I?". In relation to myself, in relation to others. The second is "What do I mean to myself?" in relation to myself and to others.

In the normal course of events, we rarely ask ourselves these questions. Instead we concentrate on function. Functioning is basic to living, starting with our bodies upon which we depend for survival and are immediately aware when they are diseased. A healthy body implies an intact brain which is in some way essentially related to consciousness, perception, speech, memory, judgement, reasoning. Damaged brains are associated with disturbance of all these functions which, between them, provide a major contribution to what is known as sanity. Between them these functions are essential for living and work.

We have now assembled the commonly accepted ingredients for functioning, taking great care not to fall into the trap of identifying brain with mind, a perennial philosophical issue of no immediate concern in this paper. For equipped as we are with mature, fully functioning bodies of different size and shape and "minds" of variable intelligence, we are capable of physiological and social survival.

We can work, earn our living, slide up and down the social scale of power and authority, tackle challenges, make discoveries, and apply logic to all sorts of issues. We have got the description of the outer self, of the social mask. Society has invested this outer self with its own priorities and values. It rewards physical and intellectual prowess with money, prizes, status; it makes use of the rest according to their capacity to which they adapt; it tolerates the incapable but not completely, for on this basis the incapable, be they young or mentally or physically defective, old, useless and unproductive, have no logical basis, no functional rationale in this framework. Those who are poor in function or lack some quality arbitrarily chosen, have no meaning and there is always a danger that this view will prevail in part or as a whole and bring forth a holocaust, a human aberration like that of Hitler and the Jews.

At this point it would seem that I am heading straight for the diminution of the significance of physical and intellectual functioning. And, despite its apparent absurdity, when so much human affirmation depends on these two characteristics, I am doing precisely this.

I am perfectly aware that the body, with its marvellous capacity to experience pleasure, give forth life, achieve new records of speed and strength, and the intellect with its unique power to perceive beauty, to be imaginative and contribute to abstract and logical thought combine to produce a concept of man placed in a social order which provides us with our daily sense of identity. I am equally aware that bodies and minds together are capable of experiencing and inflicting pain, cruelty, wars, chaos, suffering, error, disorder and destruction. One set of events we denote by the word good: the other with the word bad.

Physical and mental functioning can certainly give us capacities which form the infrastructure of the personality, but for its ultimate significance we have to turn to values. We invest capacities, actions, results with values. These values are constructed on various principles but they are not primarily self generated. We depend on the collective and inherited wisdom of the past for the standards and values of the society we live in. They are given to us but if we feel strongly enough and are capable of influencing large sections of the community, we can change them. Part of our identity thus depends on the degree to which we conform to the values of the society in which we live. We are affirmed in the social order by conforming to established expectations or, in rare instances, by creating new standards, the work of prophets and geniuses and sometimes their indistinguishable brothers and sisters, the "insane".

The answer to the two questions "who am I?" and "what do I mean to myself?" thus depends partially on this social and moral affirmation but ultimately it depends on neither. Ultimately it depends on an experience over which we have no control whatsoever; namely, the meaning and value we acquired from our parents, or parent surrogates, acquired at a time we had no choice about the donors of our personal meaning or little capacity to change the direction and/or quality of our personal affirmation received at their hands.

Nobody has ever questioned the importance of childhood. The helplessness of the child makes its physical dependence on others obvious to all. With the advance of educational instruction, the privileges of learning, first confined to the few, have become universal rights. In this century, and particularly in the last few decades, we are beginning to realise that beyond body and mind there lies the uniqueness of the I-Thou relationship which is first forged in the womb and assumes overwhelming importance (depending which school of thought is followed) somewhere in the first six to twelve years.

The Importance of Childhood

In the first part of this paper I drew attention to the fact that in the ordinary course of events we are aware of ourselves and others in terms of our adult bodies and intellects, functioning in a society steeped with a sense of social class, status, power and authority. In this largely impersonal world, feelings of a personal nature do not stand out as easily measurable or discernible elements. Yet if we look at the world of the deprived, we see repeatedly men and women whose common characteristics are feelings of alienation with themselves and others. They feel unwanted − they lack self esteem, are easily susceptible to criticism, find it hard to trust themselves or others, find it difficult to give or receive loving feelings and to retain them, leading to sustained difficulties in initiating or maintaining productive relationships with others.

Restoration to physical well-being can give the physically deprived health. Financial support can ameliorate material hardship and improved educational opportunities can potentiate the available intellectual resources. But the key to personal acceptance, to personal affirmation which is the pivot of physical and intellectual function lies in the unique experiences of the child in the hands of the most powerful affirmers, its parents, in the course of the early years.

Realisation of Potential

No attempt will be made here to enlarge on the theories of the development of human personalities which will be found in the appropriate textbooks. Sufficient to say that part of the picture is self evident, at least in our society. Everybody knows or is soon informed − if they do not − of the normal pattern of physical growth. In the absence of disease, malnutrition or wilful damage this is reasonably easily achieved.

Intellectual growth does not fit so easily into self evident categories.

The need for mental stimulation, the provision of opportunities in suitable surroundings, the balance between learning, in the old-fashioned sense of acquiring knowledge, and the need for spontaneous, experimenting, self manipulating programmes, the pursuit and satis-faction of curiosity and adventure, the encouragement of the imagination, all these and other variables become far more complicated than the measurement of height, weight and the checking of hearing, sight, teeth, etc.

Emotional growth is of course the least clearly charted territory which involves basically the following factors. The child has to develop its sense of trust, autonomy, initiative, to cope with feelings of shame, guilt, rivalry, ambivalence (having negative and positive feelings towards the same person at different or at the same times), to handle its anger, anxiety and destructiveness, to learn to repair when it is damaging, and, in brief, learn that its goodness or its positive value is greater than its badness or its negative, damaging side.

In order to achieve all this, to realise its potential, it depends utterly on its innate resources, those of the parents and their response. The response of the parents is usually called care. I want to distinguish between caring and affirmation.

Caring

I see caring as consisting of the following components. First of all the provision, in so far as it is humanly possible, of the ingredients for growth: physical care in health and in illness, the provision of intellectual stimulants within parental limits at home, supplemented by school, in an environment which provides stability, continuity and reliability for emotional growth. Provided these conditions exist in the presence of at least a minimum awareness of the unfolding phases of growth so that each phase is recognized and handled with at least minimum regard to its needs, care is said to exist. But care is only one part of the process of stimulating growth and now I want to describe the concept of affirmation which, as I said at the very beginning of this paper, is dependent entirely on feelings.

Affirmation and Helplessness

We all start life in a state of helplessness. The very smallness and helplessness of the human infant is a stimulus to its protection and throughout life helplessness evokes the desire to assist. But the state of smallness makes the infant and child totally dependent on the good will of the adult. How this good will is dispensed is a vital matter of affirmation. For no one should enter this world as a beggar. Life is not only sacrosanct when it comes to the matter of abortion. The helpless baby has a right to feel that life is not a concession granted to it by

157

kind permission of its parents. It has a claim to independence and value and this it can only learn by the way it feels it is treated. Erikson writes of the first year of life as the year in which the sense of trust begins to develop. This is absolutely true. But in the sense of affirmation it is also the beginning of the parental proclamation that life is yours, not mine.

Affirmation, Separation and Achievement

This sense of autonomy exhibits itself from the very moment of birth when the physical separation establishes the beginnings of two models, the world of "me" and the world of the "not me". Far too often this early world has been constructed and experienced as the world of the permissible and the forbidden. Development largely dependent on authoritarian principles has left many people with a sense only of that which is permissible or forbidden. Affirmation in fact aims to stress the enlarging acquisition of separate existence and achievement. It is the purpose of affirmation to detect the earliest sign of the arrival of a new skill, be it standing, crawling, climbing, walking, articulating, putting sentences together, handling objects, etc. encouraging their development with just the right amount of help and giving credit of the achievement where it belongs. Affirmation is not only facilitation for achievement, even more important it is the imparting of the sense that the achievement rightly belongs to the source of origin. Affirmation is achievement by an enlargement of self and a reduction of infantile dependence.

Affirmation and the Sense of Goodness

The parents rejoice in the enlargement of the child's world. They take pride in its achievement. The child shares in this joy but affirmation requires that it learns to feel that this achievement belongs to it and it is good. Goodness has been associated for so long with authoritarian systems, which valued conformity and obedience, that we have forgotten the basic need of the child to realise through feeling that its goodness rests on the sum total of the confirmation of each and every experience, be they feelings, thoughts, words or actions. Here it is utterly dependent on parents and others round it to confirm a sense of its value by investing its activity with intrinsic worth.

We have lived in a society which has inherited thousands of years of tradition of negative reinforcement. Goodness was built on avoiding "the forbidden" which was clearly prescribed by rules and regulations, violation of which meant punishment which was designed to help the growth of goodness. Growing through a journey of don'ts is very different from growing through a journey of highlighted achievement which, from the most minute to the largest experience, is hailed and repeatedly given the feeling of being of value and good.

Affirmation and the Sense of Badness

'But that is utopian nonsense' will be certainly murmured by some-one. Children have the capacity to irritate, annoy, damage. The baby's crying keeps the parents awake; its mess needs clearing up; their teeth bite the breast and hurt; they crawl and pull things down which break; they are attention seeking, disobedient, noisy, disorderly and so on. As a parent I can say amen to all this, either from personal or second-hand experience and so can all parents. What is beginning to happen now, possibly for the first time, is that we listen to what our children think of *us* as parents. The facts are that both have shortcomings which need correcting. The child needs to learn to delay immediate gratification, to be aware of the needs of others in preference to itself, to distinguish between real gold and all that glitters, to recognize complexity, per-severance, persistence, to cope with pain, disappointment and crisis without feeling that all is lost.

But in learning about all these marks of maturity it has to preserve its own sense of goodness, and for this, once again, it depends entirely on the quality of feelings it experiences at the hands of its parents.

At this stage of its life goodness and badness are deeply personal experiences because they involve the gain and loss of the most important aspects of living, namely closeness and approval from the most significant people in life — the parents. Both closeness and distance, approval and disapproval have a quality in which every moment is an eternity of paradise or hell.

Affirmation in these circumstances needs to assist in clarifying that which is truly damaging to self or others. The action is stamped with disapproval, the person is somehow contaminated with it. But the person retains a personal significance greater than the contamination of the action and must be given the opportunity to make reparation without loss of basic goodness. The sense of shame or guilt and the attendant fear must never be large enough to enforce a denial of responsibility. Fear ultimately contributes to lying but beyond fear is our inability to accept our own badness and, in these circumstances, we must find scapegoats. It is everybody's responsibility except ours. This never happens when personal affirmation in childhood ensured that the sense of badness was never larger than the sense of goodness and never threatened our personal significance in the eyes of those who mattered to us.

Affirmation and Personal Significance

From the moment of birth onwards we become aware that our life is related to a significant other. The level of awareness does not assume certainty until about the third or fourth month of life when, according to Bowlby, a unique bond of personal attachment is formed between mother and child. Here we come to a cornerstone of the experience of affirmation. No one interested in this subject can afford not to read Bowlby's massive work on attachment and loss of which the second volume has just appeared. I consider these studies as of historic significance and part of the permanent edifice of human psychology.

It is through the formation of this one-to-one bond that human relationship assumes the personal significance it does. This bond is primarily served by instinctual systems of sound, vision and touch. The mother recognises the baby and communicates with it before speech or reason enters the relationship, simply by hearing its cry, seeing its appearance and the feel of its touch. The baby reciprocates without words or reason and recognises mother by her face, the sounds she makes and her touch.

These are the essentials of physical affirmation in personal relationships and provide the background for all future personal relationships as well as the anxiety, suffering and mourning when the bond is broken.

Within these bonds and all other bonds we form later on with father, siblings and relatives, we come to know the meaning of being recognized or ignored, of feeling wanted or rejected, appreciated or not by the quality of the signals we receive.

Self-Possession

We can now see and summarise the outline of affirmation in childhood. It is a process for which we are largely dependent on parents in whom we place the trust to safeguard our gradual separation, differentiation and the investment of our gradual expansion of potential, physically, intellectually and emotionally with a sense of intrinsic goodness. This goodness first derives its validity from our parents because a personal bond was created between ourselves and them which invested us with personal meaning in giving us recognition, acceptance, appreciation.

All this would be of no avail if at the end of childhood we did not have enough awareness of our separate and differentiated sense of ourselves in which we felt that our bodies, minds and feelings were our own possession and invested with sufficient positive meaning to negotiate the next phase of our life, namely our adolescence and marriage.

Marriage – The Adult Affirmation

Adolescence:

On an average people get married in their early twenties. Between leaving school and this period, adolescence intervenes. It is an enormous subject which is not our main concern today. But it is a time of life when the cycle of human deprivation shows itself by the presence of young men and women who fail to detach themselves from their families, feel trapped in a dependence on parents they resent, are confused about their working capacity, what they want to do, their sexual capacity to attract. They sit defiantly or with an air of abandonment in front of one demanding an answer to the meaning of life which they are convinced has none. They are classical demonstrations of the failure to possess themselves minimally and at a time when society has decided that they must control their own destiny with the minimum of external support (such as army service, apprenticeships or supervision), far from being drop-outs they are still waiting to enter, to drop in to their identity.

The most pathetic and potentially most dangerous answer is to go through a marriage ceremony at 16, 17 or 18, in hope that a ring on the third finger, a change of surname, abode and role will give the missing sense of affirmation, of identity. It is not surprising that this age group has the highest marital breakdown rate.

Marriage and Future Expectations:

But the overwhelming majority negotiate the crisis and enter marriage. Traditionally we have thought of marriage in terms of a monogamous union, characterised by sexual exclusiveness and permanency, for the purpose of procreation and rearing of children. Contemporary societies throughout the world are challenging this Judaeo-Christian model, if the divorce rate and marital breakdown in general is a crucial index.

The prophets of gloom as usual have the answer. What can we expect with sexual slackness, loose living, no moral discipline. With them there can be no debate – they have identified the problem, they *know* the answers. Back to the good old days.

Whatever else we can do, we cannot go back exactly to anything and so it is important to interpret the present upheaval. And one answer returns. Given that material standards have improved, men and women are looking for a deeper layer of personal fulfilment which brings us back to caring and affirmation in marriage which I will distinguish as I did in the experience of childhood.

Marriage and Caring:

When we think of marriage, normally we go through a sequence which involves a couple starting at the church or with a legal ceremony, going off to their honeymoon, setting up a home and rearranging their lives to complement each other. Despite many changes, in which the wife may remain at work initially, or return later, it is still considered the husband's responsibility to be the main provider and therefore to continue at work. Despite many changes in which the husband assumes household duties rarely entertained before, it is the wife who has the main role of supervising the care of the home. Caring in marriage does in fact refer to making sure that the husband provides adequately and the wife supervises effectively so that the basic material security and comfort of living is maintained. For a long time – and even today – these principal roles of the spouses were the main basis on which the relationship existed but something is altering fundamentally and the alteration takes us to affirmation.

Affirmation and the one-to-one Relationship:

The gradual elimination of the socially but not biologically fixed roles of husband/provider and head of household, wife/housekeeper and childbearer, has meant that the husband-wife relationship can assume the characteristics of the intimacy of the one-to-one emotional relationship of parent and child. I consider this to be the most important change in marriage today with immense personal consequences. In the past attention was first given to the ability of the couple to fulfil their expected roles. Love might or might not enter the relationship but it was not essential. Today marriage assumes usually the second unique one-to-one relationship with many of the attributes and characteristics of the first, between parent and child. In this one-to-one relationship the spouses become the principal agents by which they give to each other the affirmation of recognition, acceptance and appreciation and many marriages are breaking down because there may be care but no such personal affirmation.

Oneness and Separateness

In the parent-child relationship the child needs to gradually separate and differentiate its unique self. In marriage affirmation requires that the spouses invest each other with a continuing sense of their own separateness and yet can become one, fuse without losing the sense of their own individuality.

It is here that so much of the battle between the sexes is fought. The need for the wife to feel that she is not absorbed, dwindling merely into an extension of her husband, is vital. The need to continue with her profession, her work, or, in the absence of either, to retain the originality of her thought, initiative, personal contribution are all part of her personal affirmation. Without losing the personal sense of uniqueness, spouses give to each other the fruits of their experience and inevitably imitate, adapt, take from each much which appears to make them one. But this closeness must never become one of infantile dependence so that the withdrawal of one leaves the other helpless. The fusion of two separate and growing selves is an expression of mature

162

dependence in which the giver never absorbs the receiver, and the receiver does not receive for the sake of survival only. In the cycle of human deprivation we see men and women who cannot live without dominating or the receiver cannot survive without helpless dependence and many incomplete variations of these basic patterns.

Affirmation and Growth:

I have just referred to growth, a concept now very different from childhood. Now the growth is no longer primarily physical nor intellectual but in both instances affirmation gives the opportunity for the further development of available resources. For this the couple need each other's inspiration, reassurance, facilitation, in brief, support. Either can pursue athletic interests or acquire new skills in every possible new field. The return of women to colleges, or to professional work, indeed to any work, often requires that deep inside them they have the support of their husband who appreciates the use of their talents, often making sacrifices in his timetable. She too may have to make sacrifices for his further advances at work or outside it.

Here we have special instances of personal growth in physical and intellectual skills. One area in which growth never ceases until our dying moment is in the expansion of our awareness of ourselves. From the time of the Greeks the advice of knowing ourselves has been proclaimed. Socrates showed to others how little they really knew and this was the beginning of wisdom. Wisdom has often been depicted in terms of intellectual acquisition of knowledge and this, as we have seen, is part of it. But there is much more to it and for this we need another person whom we can trust to reveal the parts of ourselves which truly expand our personality.

It is easy, only too easy, to point out to another person those aspects of their personality which annoy us and to imply that they are bad or causing us inconvenience. When this is coupled with the conviction that it is good to point out people's faults, so that they correct them, we are back in the familiar parent-child picture.

I stressed there that the parental responsiblity was not to ignore the intrinsic limitations of childhood but to bear in mind that the goodness of the child must remain uppermost for the purpose of affirmation. The same principles apply between spouses. They need each other's affirmation about most things they do. Our goodness is not a static quality; it needs constant renewal and we depend on our spouse, perhaps more than anybody else, to affirm the goodness of all our activities.

Once again there will be murmurs of 'Utopian nonsense' especially when we think of the thousand and one defects of our spouses. And yet when we reflect on the precious moments of our relationship we can perceive those moments when our limitations were picked up, neither exaggerated nor reinforced, but we were given the opportunity to correct them without losing our self esteem. This is very different from correction based on guilt as a catalyst or, even worse, the maintenance of our identity on the strength of the weakness of each other. Sometimes the affirmation does not depend on the elimination of faults but is in fact the revelation of a new feature in our make up which hitherto was unconscious. Affirmation now becomes a positive enrichment, an expanding discovery or a sense of completion.

For such affirmation we need to have empathy; to be aware of the inner world of our partner. To detect what is there and the changes which continue throughout life, which need the sensitivity and confirmation of another person who cares sufficiently to bring forth and clarify that which is blurred and confused but important inside us. To use medical terms, spouses need less surgical skills which cut things out and more midwifery which brings things out, assist in giving birth to each other's inner world.

Affirmation and Healing:

I have referred to our traditional conditioning of promoting growth by pointing out faults in others, acknowledging them in ourselves and through shame or guilt changing for the better. Change can certainly take place in this way but a large component of this change has fear as its basis and fear is not the best agent for growth or healing.

The intimacy of the contemporary marital relationship not only exposes the most minute nuances of the inner world but also provides the most unique opportunity for healing – healing in the way that Freud first discovered in psychoanalysis. In psychoanalysis what is essentially established is a relationship of emotional intimacy and trust in which the therapist receives the distorted feelings of the first relationship between child and parent and provides a second opportunity for new feelings to develop.

Spouses provide exactly this possibility for each other. The most recurrent need for healing appertains to feelings and emotions. Men and women come to marriage with the wounds of the first relationship upon them. The common wounds are excessive dependence, anxiety, insecurity, lack of self esteem, an undifferentiated self lacking in confidence, the inability to feel, to give and to receive feelings, to retain them, low threshold to frustration with exaggerated aggression and an excessive capacity to hurt, devalue and damage. Each of these wounds can be healed if the spouse responds with patience, care, does not retaliate and thus gives a new experience of acceptance, meaning, encouragement, reassurance and confidence to the partner. Needless to say, when both partners have nothing but wounds to offer each other, the survival of the relationship is at risk but when as usual the strength of one complements the weakness of the other, there is plenty of opportunity for healing.

Sexual Act:

Marriage has one act which is forbidden to the parent-child relationship. What is incest to them is perhaps the single most important affirmation to the married couple. Each and every act has this potential. In the act there is the same physical closeness as in the mother-baby closeness and, therefore, evokes the same element of trust. In its absence, in the presence of anxiety and tension, some of the commonest sexual disorders occur. In this physical closeness, through the medium of touch and fusion, the couple affirm each other by denoting, if not actually verbalising, the feeling that they recognise, want, appreciate each other as the most important person in their life. Here is repeated acceptance, investing each other through the body with the essential goodness of each other's being which is central to affirmation. In the sexual act the couple donate totally each to the other and thus affirm each other's sexual identity and personal significance. It is because the act can mean so much, in that it can combine caring, relief of sexual tension, growth, healing, in fact all the ingredients of affirmation that it has been invested with the quality of signifying the uniqueness of a personal bond through exclusiveness. It is because the sexual act has such richness, which is fully effective in one relationship at a time that its random use deprives it of the fullness of its potential.

Children:

We are accustomed to think of the sexual act leading to procreation. Quite clearly in the future man will control procreation biologically to the point where the number of children may be tied to about the same number of sexual acts and for the rest sexual intercourse will provide the affirmation which clearly it possesses and which can be clearly understood in our day. Nevertheless children are central to the affirmation of the couple. But we can see now that if the spouses can continue to provide fullness of meaning for each other's identity, the child has the best chance of receiving those characteristics which will affirm it and continue the cycle of human affirmation rather than deprivation. The relationship of the spouses indubitably comes before child-bearing.

Permanency and Relationship:

Thus we have now come to the full circle of the cycle of human affirmation. Each relationship begins with the presence of a significant other, first the parents then later the spouses become the significant other to each other. In both instances the deepest layer of affirmation requires a relationship of trust and closeness in which the physical, psychological, intellectual and social aspects of each are identified, encouraged to grow and affirmed by feelings which invest and maintain the total goodness of the person. In the very nature of the process, permanency in the form of continuity, reliability and predictability are essential for the realisation of the goal of affirmation. A great deal of marital breakdown is the failure of spouses to provide for each other the essentials of this affirmation which is increasingly being part of the expectation of life. Christianity has a responsibility to give the lead in this matter.

The Place of Faith

Affirmation by faith:

At this point I will conclude by introducing for the first time the word Christianity. People sometimes ask me how my faith fits in with a whole address in which the familiar language of God, prayer, grace, sacraments is missing. Since it is my contention that often these words are used in a vacuum of ignorance about the human reality they are meant to transform, I make it a point of first establishing the human component. It is a familiar idea that grace builds on nature and Christianity has paid a heavy price for ignoring man's changing consciousness of his nature which has taken place in this century. Man cannot respond to grace if his essential nature is ignored by the Church.

It was my deliberate intention to show that there is nothing in the principles of human affirmation that cannot be recognized by our humanist friends who decry the need for God or faith. The point of my departure would be the quality of implementation of this cycle without the presence of faith. I believe that faith, particularly the faith that belongs to the Judaeo-Christian tradition, can make a fundamental difference to the realisation of the goal of affirmation because it is a faith based on love, not on law, and love is at the heart of this cycle.

Significant Other:

Faith begins in the awareness and initiation of a relationship in baptism with the Significant Other we call God. Now we can see why Freud reduced religion and the sense of God to a simple projection of our infantile dependency needs. Since the whole of our life is dependent on a significant other, we can easily construct a fictional supreme other who continues to meet our infantile needs. The first element of the affirmation of true faith is an awareness that experiences God as a truly independent, self-revealing identity who is the Significant Other of all creation and of all of us because He exists and chose to reveal

166

himself, first in the covenant he made with Israel and then through His only Son, Jesus Christ.

Creation:

In a reference full of psychological meaning St. John reminds us that we love because God loved us first. In faith, the beginning lies with God, who expressed the fullness of his love in creation. The two accounts of creation will be found in the first two chapters of Genesis. The points I want to draw attention to are that man was created in the image of God, that this creation had a sexual differentiation and that the second account of creation ends with the words – 'This is why a man leaves his father and mother and joins himself to his wife and they become one body. Now both of them were naked, the man and his wife, but they felt no shame in front of each other.' (Gen 2; vv 24, 25) Thus sexuality and marriage are at the very centre of God's revelation of himself in creation. His self revelation is expressed in man and his affirmation of man is found in relationship, the creative relationship of man to woman and both back to himself.

Jesus Christ:

But Paul or the author of Ephesians reminds us, from the beginning of time God's plan included something else stated in one simple phrase.

'Before the world was made, he chose us, chose us in Christ, to be holy and apostles, and to live in love in his presence, determined that we should become his adopted sons through Jesus Christ.'

Eph. 1: 3-4

Ultimately the fullness of affirmation will be found in and through Christ. Now it is interesting to note that Christ's own affirmation took place without marriage. All those who wish to dedicate themselves and live their lives in the single state may find the principles of affirmation as outlined in this paper a bit disconcerting. Is there no affirmation without marriage? Clearly there is: but there is no affirmation without the presence of a significant other, a point of the utmost importance in the restructuring of religious life. Christ was affirmed by his Father at his baptism.

"As soon as Jesus was baptised he came up from the water and suddenly the heavens opened and he saw the Spirit of God descending like a dove and coming down on him. And a voice spoke from heaven. "This is my Son, the Beloved, my favour rests on him."

Matthew 3: 16-17

All the essentials of affirmation, trust, recognition, acceptance, appreciation and confirmation of goodness are present and are repeated in the Transfiguration (Matthew 17: 1-8). This is not to say that Christ's relationship with the Father was confined to these moments. His relationship was continuous and mediated through prayer, the language of awareness of the Significant Other.

Fullness and Self Possession:

Affirmation, we have noted, is the ultimate process of self-possession in that the individual is aware of the fullness of being and accepts it all as intrinsically good. I have indicated elsewhere that psychologically this is the state of Christ's personality which allowed him to accept all others because there was nothing in him that he was not aware of or would not accept: hence there was nothing in others he could not recognize or needed to reject except sin. This fullness is described in various Pauline epistles and summarised in Colossians:

'Before anything was created, he existed
and he holds all things in Unity.'

Col. 1: 17

The Church:

But all that he holds in unity is to be found in his body which he has bestowed on us as the Church. This is not the Church of rules and regulations, of arguments and quarrels. These are its necessary human manifestations but these details blur the reality. The Church is all of us, the body of the people of God living in and through Christ's body which the author of Ephesians states to be the:

'Fullness of him who fills the whole creation.'

Eph. 1: 23

By participation in the Church, in its life and therefore in the life of Christ our distinguishing characteristics of faith emerge. Our awareness is no longer of the human significance of others, they become important because they and we are all living in the presence of the most significant other of all, Jesus Christ, and Paul's prayer to the Ephesians is that:-

'He may live in your hearts through faith, and then planted in love and built on love, you will with all the saints have the strength to grasp the breadth and the length, the height and the depth, until knowing the love of Christ, which is beyond all knowledge, you are filled with the utter fullness of God.'

Eph. 3: 17-19

168

The Church and Home:

But how, may we ask? The Church is a reality, but we are mostly aware of the human tensions in it, the concreteness of the rules and regulations we should follow, a sacramental life we believe in but find difficult to experience its reality. How are we to experience the fullness of Christ in his Church? The sacraments are one means. And within them, (and here is the distinguishing mark of Catholicism) one of them, marriage, which is embraced by the overwhelming majority of human beings, brings the Church into their life.

For in the peroration about marriage at the end of the letter to the Ephesians, its author brings his concept of the Church, the body of Christ, right up to each and every home, family and marriage. The union of husband and wife and their relationship to each is compared to the union of Christ and the Church and every marriage becomes a "little Church" in which the affirmation of its members shares and participates in the affirmation of Christ for the Church. Marriage remains central in the original revelation of God to man in creation and in its confirmation in the life and death of His only Son.

The conclusion of the Cycle of Human Affirmation:

And that for the Christian is the true conclusion of the cycle of human affirmation. The meeting and union of human persons create an atmosphere for growth, healing and ultimate affirmation in the various phases of the cycle of human development. The phases meet and align themselves with Jesus Christ whose one Body is the Church also growing, healing and affirming its members in love.

INDEX

171

173